YOU'RE ON FIRE, IT'S FINE

YOU'RE ON FIRE, IT'S FINE

Effective Strategies for Parenting Teens
with Self-Destructive Behaviors

KATIE K. MAY

YOU'RE ON FIRE, IT'S FINE
Effective Strategies for Parenting Teens with Self-Destructive Behaviors

FIRST EDITION

ISBN 978-1-5445-4559-2 *Hardcover*
      978-1-5445-4558-5 *Paperback*
      978-1-5445-4560-8 *Ebook*
      978-1-5445-4549-3 *Audiobook*

To my teen. The world became bigger than the pain inside me when I knew you were on the way. Breaking the chain of dysfunction is my greatest gift to you. ❤

Contents

Introduction

It's Not Fine

THE AFTERMATH OF MY PARENTS' DIVORCE WHEN I WAS ten set the stage for my tumultuous teenage years. My mom disappeared from our daily lives and suddenly I had to juggle adult responsibilities—playing the role of housekeeper, cook, and pseudo-parent to my younger sister. My emotional turmoil during this time was intense, yet in our home, emotions were dismissed or entirely ignored. The pain of my mom's absence was palpable, but never acknowledged. Even worse, any feelings I expressed about missing her were met with punishment instead of understanding or support.

Fast forward to my teenage years. I was a bigger kid facing even more significant challenges, with a dad who still hadn't figured out parenting beyond his old default of demands and threats. After a particularly painful breakup, my depression surged, anchoring me to my bed as I wept for two whole days. My dad, totally out of his depth, called in my Aunt "TT" to support me. She sat on the edge of my bed, just listening. No one seemed to have any clear idea of how to help or what to do.

Self-harm became my go-to escape. Razors concealed in bathroom cabinets and broken mirrors, their shards repurposed as tools for self-inflicted pain, became my means of coping. Imagine a teenager, so overwhelmed with sadness, breaking a mirror with her fist to turn its pieces against herself. When I reached out to my dad after hurting myself, his unexpectedly comforting responses paradoxically fueled my self-destructive behavior. These moments twistedly validated my pain: they saw, acknowledged, and felt my suffering.

My support system did little to mitigate the shortcomings in my dad's parenting. The message from my extended family was clear: I didn't fit in. "Stop being weird," they'd say. "Why are you wearing that?" "Don't be a know-it-all." "You're too sensitive." These remarks were constant.

I survived by numbing myself with scars and substances, avoiding the need to feel. The expression of my emotions was "not right," leading me to believe that experiencing them was inherently wrong. Feeling unwanted and out of place, I doubled down on self-destructive habits.

I would do anything to escape the pain. Shoplifting, sneaking out at night, smoking weed—I was desperate to extinguish the fire inside me. Impulsive actions provided momentary relief and elicited concerned attention from my dad, which I always wanted, no matter how misguided his reactions were.

My life took a drastic turn when I unexpectedly became pregnant at twenty-six. The prospect of bringing a new life into the world put into perspective that my purpose was greater than the pain inside me. I recognized the need to heal and to disrupt the generational cycle of pain.

My pregnancy marked the beginning of my journey back

to myself, as I gradually began healing through therapy, reflection, reading, and writing. My commitment to personal growth took me back to school for clinical counseling, which enriched my understanding of human behavior, family dynamics, and breaking unhealthy patterns.

As my child grew, my family did too. However, inviting my mother to my wedding caused a rift. My grandmother severed ties with me, resulting in a twelve-year estrangement from my extended family. This separation reignited the intense feelings of loneliness and rejection I experienced in my childhood. But when grieving gave way to acceptance, this distance became a gift. Away from the family where I never felt like I belonged, I finally found myself.

I channeled my experiences into founding Creative Healing, a place that helps hundreds of teens each week with self-acceptance and emotion regulation, something my younger self desperately needed. I also created a home for my own teen, where authenticity is not just accepted but celebrated.

This book is my way of sharing the lessons learned through my transformation with you. Together, we'll explore ways to create positive change at home, with skillful parenting practices that benefit the whole family.

WHO IS THIS BOOK FOR?

As a therapist who specializes in teen self-harm, it's not uncommon for me to work with parents who feel sad and hopeless about their teen's behavior. They may have tried six to ten therapists, but nothing is working. They're at the point of considering sending their child to a residential program, and they're feeling guilty, helpless, and uncertain about what to do next.

By the time many families find our center, they've already experienced years of intense emotions and behaviors at home and have already tried tons of treatments and therapies. Often, they've received a lot of contradictory advice from different professionals too.

And none of it with any long-term lasting effects.

Parenting a teen can be challenging, and it's natural to feel overwhelmed and unsure of how to move forward when things aren't going well. It's not always easy, but with patience, persistence, and a willingness to try new approaches (including looking inward and changing your own patterns), it is possible to find solutions and create positive change at home. And that's what I hope to impart to you in these pages.

The teens and families I work with go from self-destruction and deep depression to coping with confidence and feeling competent, without years of therapy, even if it feels like they've tried it all before. I wrote this book to expand the scope of teen support services beyond the greater Philadelphia area, where my amazing team and I continue to help teens learn to love themselves unconditionally, while also learning to improve and become more skillful in the process.

There's no gratitude greater for me than the ironclad belief I've fostered that I'm not weird, bad, wrong, or different for being myself. In fact, it's what got me here. And when you can shed the layers you've built to protect yourself and tap into your willingness to self-reflect and do the inner work, I can guide you and your teen there too.

A ROADMAP FOR PARENTING TEENS
WITH OVERWHELMING EMOTIONS

Listen up, buttercup...yelling doesn't work. (If it did, you would have stopped by now!) Neither do strict rules that force teens to comply without understanding why. Oh, and giving in and saving teens from their feelings? Nope, not that one either.

It's tough stuff to understand and address your teen's impulsive behaviors. These behaviors, however, serve a purpose, and by understanding their function, you can better understand how to address them. One way to do this is by building empathy for your teen's experiences. By seeing things from their perspective and recognizing the challenges they may face, you can improve your relationship and decrease your own feelings of anger, frustration, and fear. I'm here to guide you through the skills needed to do this.

Before we make changes, however, we've got to dig into the "why" of what's going on. We'll cover the root function of problematic behaviors in teenagers. My goal is to help you get to the core of these issues and find solutions that will prevent them from becoming bigger problems down the road. We'll talk about how to make sense of your teenager's behaviors and create opportunities for positive change within your home environment.

The Biosocial Theory can also be a helpful framework for understanding the root cause of your teen's difficulties in managing their emotions. This theory recognizes that both nature (biology and genetics) and nurture (environment and upbringing) play a role in our behavior and emotions. By gaining insight into this nature and nurture dynamic, you can develop a better understanding of your teen's behavior and the power you have to positively influence change at home.

We'll dig into everyday mindfulness to help you better understand and navigate your emotions. By learning to tune into your own experiences and actions, as well as how you and your teen influence each other, you will gain a greater understanding of the automatic judgments that fuel painful emotions. By shifting to a nonjudgmental stance and developing language that helps you become more mindful and objective, you will create a space for positive change in your relationships.

In this book, we will discuss in detail the development of self-regulation, which is a key skill. By learning how to manage escalating crises at home and how to prevent them from happening in the first place, you can create a more peaceful and supportive environment for everyone. This involves understanding what triggers you and mastering exactly what to do to manage these triggers effectively.

Radical Acceptance is required for parenting a teenager with big emotions, or really any teen. It's important to acknowledge the grief and other hard feelings that can come with this experience, and to develop skills that help you drop the struggle and nurture yourself with compassion. You will build the strength and energy needed to support your teenager rather than resenting them or feeling hopeless about the future.

By gaining the scripts and skills to halt emotional escalation and encourage flexibility with validation, you'll learn to create a more supportive and understanding environment for your teen. This is the first step in creating positive change. Our words and actions can have an immense impact on our teenagers' behavior. I'll share with you what to say and do to validate your teenager, as well as what not to do that might make the situation worse. I'll also provide you with words and phrases that can help to soothe your teen's emotions, all based on brain science and proven to be effective.

We'll review the formula for growing positive and preferred behaviors while decreasing and phasing out unhelpful, ineffective, and unsafe behaviors. By learning the principles of behaviorism and creating a plan of action, you will work toward creating a more harmonious home environment.

You can repair your relationship with your teen, no matter what you've been through. By learning the skills to rebuild step-by-step and focusing on creating greater harmony with one interaction at a time, you will work toward a stronger and more positive relationship with your teenager.

My promise to you is you will walk away with a clear understanding of what to do and say to help your teen regulate their emotions before they become problematic behaviors. We don't want you doing damage control. We want you orchestrating a proactive approach so you can experience a meticulously tuned system that collaboratively works for your whole family.

WHO AM I?

My dad told me growing up that there was no instruction manual for raising kids like me. So I created one. My teenage experiences with depression and self-destructive behaviors have guided me toward a profession of passion. I am proud to be one of only eleven Linehan board-certified Dialectical Behavior Therapy (DBT) clinicians in Pennsylvania, and the sole board-certified DBT specialist leading a team that specializes in adolescent care. This certification is the gold standard treatment for individuals with suicidal ideation and self-harm behaviors. I'm the owner and executive director of

Creative Healing, Teen Support Centers. We see hundreds of teenagers each week in both individual and group treatment who come to us with concerns about anxiety, depression, low self-esteem, suicidal thoughts, and self-harm behaviors. By the time they complete treatment, they're no longer acting on urges to harm themselves, they're liking themselves more, they're better connected with peers, and they have the tools for balance and stability in their moods so even when they're feeling sad or worried, they know exactly what to do to stay on track and manage challenges.

This profession is not just a career; it's my life's calling. This book therefore serves as both a personal love letter to my journey from depression to self-acceptance and a roadmap for caregivers who are raising teenagers just like I was.

My words and stories are my own and are told through the lens of my personal experiences and memories. I also share stories of teens and parents, an amalgam of all clients presented through mock client scenarios. It's easy to share without breaking confidentiality because every family I've helped has experienced something similar: emotion dysregulation, difficulty using skills, and a push for change without reality acceptance. And I share stories about parenting my teen, to show that even when you have the tools, the day-to-day will not always be easy.

This is a true story from a professional who's been there and done that. Parenting a teenager can be tough, but it doesn't have to be. I would like to help you shorten the path of struggle and skip faster to the celebration. With the right tools, you can navigate the teenage years with confidence and ease. Let me help you find those tools and empower you to be the best parent you can be for your teen.

THE TOOLS *YOU* NEED TO PARENT YOUR TEEN

Looking for a quick fix? You won't find it here. Focusing solely on your teen without taking responsibility for your own actions will make it challenging to finish this book. Unwillingness to put in the effort means you won't see results, and consequently, your teen won't change.

I invite you to read with an open mind and to consider how your thoughts, emotions, and behaviors influence your teen in your relationship with them. This book is about owning what is yours to change. It's about learning the who and how of your identity in parenting a highly emotional teen. Read, reflect, and practice. Take notes, but don't just leave them on the page; put them into action. Notice what happens when you take consistent daily steps toward your goal. You've got this. I'm rooting for you. All right...turn the page and dig in.

CHAPTER 1

⸻

Your Teen Is on Fire

TEN DAYS BEFORE CHRISTMAS, WHEN I WAS TEN YEARS old, my parents called me up to their bedroom. My mind raced as I climbed the stairs. It seemed serious. It sounded like the tone of parents who were about to tell me who the real gift-giver was on Christmas morning, a question that had been on my mind for the past month because of some rumblings at school.

Even now, I can picture them both sitting on the edge of their bed together. It was the last time they shared that space, the last time they shared a conversation that was kind, and the last time I retained the innocence of a child who still believed in Santa.

As a kid, I didn't know the impact of the word divorce. I didn't know anyone who had gone through a divorce. I had no vision of how my life would change. So I asked them what would happen next.

"Everything will be the same," they promised. "We just won't live together."

The irony is my Santa question got answered that day too. I

was lying on the floor on the far side of my bed...crying, journaling, and writing sad poetry. My dad tossed open the door and threw in a bunch of boxes and gifts, slated for my siblings.

"Here," he said matter-of-factly. "Your mother won't be here to do this. It's your job now."

I wept while I wrapped.

Christmas morning came. I remember opening a Polly Pocket playset and intentionally constructing a barrier between my emotions and reaction. Santa suddenly became a stranger, completely unfamiliar with me. And I suppose that was true. My mother wasn't there to do the shopping.

I can picture the look of desperation on my dad's face when he forced his famous Christmas quip, "What'd ya get, Kate?"

I forced a smile and feigned excitement. "Everything could stay the same," I told myself.

Days and years went by, and each passing holiday season became a reminder of my world being torn apart. Christmas meant putting up a tree and lights and celebrating what used to be a time filled with magic moments. But for me, it felt bleak and empty. I was a child tasked with creating Christmas magic while feeling shattered by what she saw behind the curtain.

And yet, to my sister five years younger, tradition was critical. Everything had to stay the same, but my mom wasn't there to carry it on. The responsibility now fell on me.

In my teen years, I acted out, sometimes toward others, but primarily in self-destructive ways.

I "ruined Christmas" again and again with my choices and behavior. I'd refuse to decorate the tree until I endured a hateful glare and words my fourteen-year-old ears will never unhear: "You decorate that tree, or I'll beat you"—the continued post-divorce default for controlling my behavior.

I wept while I decorated the tree.

My refusal to engage in family traditions, a resistance to our old rituals, was my expression of pain. Misunderstood as defiance, it only invited harsher discipline. This discipline deepened my feelings of invalidation and loneliness, leading to screaming matches and self-harm.

The painful experience of my parents' untimely separation, losing my mom as a consistent figure in my life, and the years of violence and conflict that followed disrupted my life for years to come. My "coping" came as self-destruction: self-harm and substance use. Later, as a young adult, I spent consecutive holiday seasons in rehab or jail. But despite the brief moments of intense pain triggered by events and memories year after year, these behaviors became an instant refuge—a rush of relief that allowed me to continue on without the pain inside consuming me.

We are going to break down the concept of problem behaviors as "solutions" for your teen. You'll understand how their emotions impact them and, in the end, how their impulsive behaviors, while dangerous, may actually make sense. The answer to "why" they engage in these behaviors lies in understanding Emotion Dysregulation.

REACHING THE SKILLS BREAKDOWN POINT

Emotion Dysregulation means struggling to handle and react to feelings in a balanced way. It's what happens when your emotions become too intense for your current ability to cope, reaching a point where they're too hard to manage.

When this happens, individuals focus their full time and attention on escaping painful emotions. Imagine unexpectedly losing your best friend in a tragic accident. This would be agonizingly painful. You might have urges to drink or even to deny the reality of the situation. This is your mind moving you away from something that feels unbearable for you. The same is true for your teen in moments of anguish.

Humans instinctively avoid pain because no one wants to feel bad. This instinct is not exclusive to teenagers but is especially strong in them because of their developing frontal lobes, which handle decision-making, impulse control, and understanding consequences. When you add hormonal changes and heightened emotional sensitivity to the mix, teens can be more prone to being overwhelmed by their emotions compared to adults.

When teens become overwhelmed by their emotions, they find it nearly impossible to focus on other tasks or be productive. In the therapy world, we call this "mood dependence." When life feels good, they're doing well. They're functional and engaging in life in ways that support success and social connection. But when their mood turns dark, their life revolves around removing or escaping uncomfortable emotions.

Teens may exhibit emotion-phobic tendencies. On what they consider "good" days, they steer clear of discussing triggering topics. It's as if they've developed a fear of emotions, anticipating that any feeling could turn a good day into a bad one. This avoidance is understandable because, when emotions emerge, they are intense, overwhelming, and enduring. For emotionally sensitive teenagers, avoiding emotions becomes a strategy to preserve their emotional equilibrium.

When overwhelmed by powerful emotions, we see life in black and white: "good, bad, right, or wrong." Imagine a day when your teen encountered a setback, like being reprimanded by a teacher. If you asked about their school day, they might reply that it was "awful!" Even if most of their day progressed flawlessly, that small 5 percent can dominate their perception, making them view the whole day as a disaster.

When emotions surge, the ability to become an effective problem solver disappears. During these times, our life goals, values, and thoughts of consequences tend to fade too. I regularly hear parents say, "They didn't think about the consequences. They don't even care!" But not caring is not the issue. In this state, teens are not emotionally aligned for rational thinking.

One day at school, Jamie is abruptly called out by her history teacher in front of the entire class for talking to a peer during a video lesson. Many teens could brush off being unexpectedly called out by their history teacher as just a bad moment, but for Jamie, who's struggling with emotion dysregulation, it becomes the defining event of her day, if not her week.

After school, she skips basketball practice and withdraws to her room. When her mom gently asks about her day, Jamie exclaims, "It was the worst day ever!" Her mom, knowing about the incident from a text earlier in the day but unaware of its emotional impact on Jamie, is left baffled. Why would such a minor incident overshadow Jamie's entire day, especially when she had brought home an A on her English paper and was on track to make the varsity basketball team?

That evening, Jamie avoids her homework, dreads going to school the next day, and even contemplates dropping the history class altogether. Her emotions have taken the driver's seat, pushing aside rational thoughts and the ability to problem-solve. She's in a space where her feelings color her entire perspective. When her father tries to talk to her about future college plans, she snaps, saying, "Why does it even matter?"

This is a glimpse into the world of a teen experiencing Emotion Dysregulation. A single incident, which many might consider minor, has the power to disrupt their entire emotional equilibrium, affecting their decisions, reactions, and interactions.

IMMEDIATE ACTIONS FOR ASSESSING YOUR TEEN'S SAFETY IN CRISIS SITUATIONS

Before we go further, it's essential to ensure your teen's safety. Seek immediate crisis support and professional help as it relates to your teen's life-threatening behaviors. This list provides steps to assess and respond to emergency situations competently.

1. **Ask:** "Are you thinking about killing yourself?" Saying the words is crucial, as it conveys your willingness to address the issue. Avoiding direct communication may signal to your teen that you cannot handle the situation.

2. **If Yes, Ask Further:** "Have you thought of how or when you would act on these thoughts?" The more specific the details regarding how and when, the higher the level of risk. Make sure to remove any potential tools mentioned from their immediate environment or access.

3. **Assess Intent, Ask:** "On a scale of 0 to 10, with 10 being 'I'm definitely going to act today' and 0 being 'I'm definitely not going to act today,' what number are you?" A higher number indicates a greater intent to act and a higher risk level.

4. **Stay Present:** Be there for your teen. Less talking is more effective. Engage in activities like watching a movie, taking a walk, or going for a drive together. Distraction is key when coping with high urges.

5. **Call for Help:** If necessary, call behavioral health crisis response services for immediate help. Prioritizing your teen's safety is paramount.

BIOLOGICALLY SENSITIVE INDIVIDUALS
AND EMOTION DYSREGULATION

Biologically sensitive people, in this book called *Fire Feelers*, are strongly influenced by their surroundings. They feel emotions deeply and struggle to handle their reactions and actions. Picture it as being engulfed in emotional flames. As these feelings intensify, they can take over, causing an inner blaze that feels all-consuming. For Fire Feelers, it's like being unable to extinguish a fire, no matter how much water they pour on it.

When you think about it that way, that your teenager is on fire with emotional flames—it becomes clearer how these overpowering sensations might push them toward thoughts of self-harm or even suicide. During times of extreme distress, the idea of self-harm or suicide might seem like the only way to escape their suffering. Thinking about suicide can bring a momentary sense of relief to those in pain. The thought that an escape from suffering is possible can provide comfort, especially when the current pain feels too much to bear.

As your teenager's emotions intensify, they're immediately consumed by thoughts like, "I can't handle this. It's just too much." Every action they take is driven by the desire to escape this overwhelming feeling. I'm not endorsing harmful actions but developing empathy and understanding for why your teen turns to these behaviors is critical for supporting your teen in the healing process. Imagine a pain so excruciating that death seems like the only way out. If you're reading this book, chances are this is what your teen is going through.

It's understandable that teenagers on fire with intense emotions might resort to drugs and alcohol to dull those feelings. They may engage in binging and purging or detach themselves from their emotions to numb the intensity. Coping comes in the form of self-destructive behaviors because these strategies match the intensity of the emotions that triggered them.

One afternoon, after several days of feeling left out and misunderstood by her closest friends, Sarah's emotions reached a breaking point. She felt like a storm of disappointment and confusion had been brewing within her, and now she unleashed it with an intensity she couldn't contain. As she sat alone in her room, tears streaming down her face, she whispered, "I just can't handle this anymore." The emotional turmoil became overwhelming, like an unstoppable wildfire spreading through her heart and mind.

In this moment of desperation, thoughts she had never encountered before emerged. She entertained the idea of self-harm, a potential escape from the emotional agony that seemed to have consumed her. Strangely, these thoughts provided a peculiar sense of comfort, a relief from the tormenting emotions that had been her constant companions. It was a fleeting break in the chaos, a temporary quelling of the inner inferno that had been raging.

For Sarah, these thoughts of self-harm became a coping mechanism, a way to briefly extinguish the flames of her anguish. In a world where her emotions felt too intense and misunderstood, this escape offered her a sense of control over her pain. It wasn't about seeking attention or acting out; it was an attempt to regain a sense of balance within a world that often felt overwhelmingly chaotic. Even the thought of self-harm was enough of an escape from emotional pain to bring her back to a baseline of emotional experience.

When supporting your teen in overcoming Emotion Dysregulation, remember that understanding their immense pain and
underlying emotions is the first step to breaking the cycle.
Instead of exclusively focusing on their behaviors, strive to
empathize with their experiences and the intensity of their
emotions.

POOR EMOTIONAL PROBLEM-SOLVING AND RELATIONSHIP DIFFICULTIES

Fire Feelers often struggle with solving emotional challenges
effectively. When emotions take over, they usually shift
into rigid, all-or-nothing thinking. They might say things
like, "Nothing ever works. Nobody cares about me. Everyone
hates me." If you spot these extreme statements, it's a sign
of all-or-nothing thinking. Such thought patterns often lead
to feelings of hopelessness and self-criticism. It's as if their
intense emotions consume them. In Chapter 3, we discuss this
issue further, providing you with the tools to break free from
these patterns and create room for positive change.

These extremes often lead to challenges in their relationships. If someone with Fire Feeler tendencies believes
that nobody likes them, their behavior might inadvertently
create issues, causing people to keep their distance. They could
become excessively clingy or display codependent tendencies,
such as relying heavily on others for emotional support and
validation. On the flip side, if they feel like everyone is against
them, their actions might provoke arguments. They might
even resort to passive-aggressive tactics, getting others to
confirm their belief that they're truly unlovable. These patterns can strain relationships and lead to misunderstandings.

Alex, a sixteen-year-old, struggled with a persistent belief that he was not worthy of friendship. A single, unreturned text transformed into a storm of worry, convincing him that his peers were upset with him. Desperate for reassurance, he started bombarding them with messages, inadvertently overwhelming them. In his attempt to disconfirm his fears, he unconsciously drove them away. The very actions he took to ease his anxiety ended up reinforcing his negative self-image, creating a cycle of isolation.

These intense thoughts and emotions often bring a lot of strain into relationships, especially when they lead to impulsive actions—when individuals act without considering how their feelings are driving their behaviors and the impact they're having.

Struggling to embrace their emotions, suppressing and numbing them, and engaging in all-or-nothing thinking all contribute to challenges in relationships. These difficulties culminate in a deep fear of being abandoned or rejected, along with constant worries that others don't approve of them or are passing judgment. This leads them to navigate life through the lens that they are undeserving of love and acceptance.

Fire Feelers are often keenly aware that people might distance themselves from them. In reaction, they might intensify their efforts to connect with others, going to the extent of reshaping themselves to conform to someone else's identity. For example, they might make an effort to fit in and be liked by pretending to like the same music or movies as a friend. They might flood someone with multiple texts within minutes if they don't receive an immediate response. Unfortunately, this behavior exacerbates relationship issues and drives people away. They're desperately seeking reassurance that they're valued, but this often results in them appearing overly intense, which causes others to withdraw.

THE LONELINESS OF EMOTION DYSREGULATION

When your teen is driven by intense emotions and acts without thinking, they might end up blurting out hurtful words, throwing insults, and getting involved in harmful actions. This can make it tough for people to stay by their side. Others might feel the direct impact of their behavior, or it might just be too painful for them to witness your teen hurting themselves, so they choose to step back.

In my teen years, I couldn't tolerate feedback. My identity was so fragile that the smallest of statements felt threatening to me. My friend and I now laugh about the time when we got ready together for a party. She glanced at me and said matter-of-factly, "I don't like that sweater." I could feel the anger rising in my belly, like a volcano erupting. "I don't like your face!" I quipped.

Feedback felt like rejection. And years later, this same friend estranged herself from me for years as I grappled with self-injury, substance abuse, and a litany of unsafe and unhealthy life choices. When we reconnected in adulthood as parents, she shared, "It hurt me too much to watch you self-destructing over and over. I couldn't do it anymore."

Reconnecting with my friend as adults and parents was a testament to our capacity for change and growth. It showed that with time, self-awareness, and behavioral changes, people can mend and strengthen even strained relationships.

Teens are naturally discovering their identity. It's a period of self-discovery. When this delicate self-awareness combines with their struggle with regulating emotions, forming an individual identity becomes even more challenging. They seek cues from their surroundings to define themselves and end up internalizing feedback that labels them as too much, weird, bad, wrong, or different for experiencing the emotions they feel.

Emotionally sensitive teens often carry a burdensome belief that they're worthless. They've received a lifetime of messaging that their emotions and urges are inaccurate or disproportionate to the situation at hand. Trusting themselves and their emotions becomes a challenge, impacting their interactions with others. This self-doubt can make life unbearably painful. Their peers might not grasp the depth of their emotions or the complexity of their emotional journey, resulting in a lonely and hurtful experience for them. In Chapter 6, we explore scripts and action steps designed to enhance connection. These strategies will focus on Validation, a tool for helping Fire Feelers navigate their emotional challenges and foster healthier relationships.

BREAKING THE CYCLE AND ADDRESSING THE ROOT

With Fire Feelers, the challenges they encounter can be both problems and solutions. Their impulsive or destructive behavior serves to regulate their overwhelming emotions, but it also generates its own set of problems. It's a cycle that can feel difficult to break, but it is possible. The first step toward initiating change involves understanding the profound pain your teen is contending with beneath their actions.

In my teen years, family conflict and abuse triggered extreme feelings of worthlessness and depression that followed me for years after each time the anniversary of these events occurred. I internalized my parents' behaviors and believed that something was wrong with me for having the feelings that I had. I harmed myself and numbed myself to cope with the insurmountable pain of these experiences.

Keep in mind that these thoughts, feelings, and behavior patterns don't just fade away on their own. Your teen won't just grow out of them; they might only become better at hiding them as they mature. For actual change to occur, it's essential to address the factors that keep these behaviors going—the reasons they work—and reshape the pattern accordingly. This is the basis of behaviorism, which we break down in great detail in Chapter 7, offering effective strategies for behavior management at home.

UNDERSTANDING THE WHEEL OF EMOTION DYSREGULATION

The Wheel of Emotion Dysregulation shows us how overwhelming emotions can lead to impulsive and self-destructive behaviors. Each "spoke" of the wheel shows a reaction to the emotional sensitivity that Fire Feelers may experience. This wheel is always moving, symbolizing the escalating momentum of emotion dysregulation and its effects on behavior.

Consider the difficulties your teen is experiencing. Keep in mind that their behaviors often serve as coping mechanisms in response to intense emotions. Ask yourself what emotions might drive their behaviors, and consider how these behaviors are connected to their intense feelings. Your teen's emotions blaze intensely due to their biological sensitivity. Take a moment to consider how you can find understanding of the behaviors you disapprove of and that terrify you. I understand they may be alarming and unsafe, but how can you make sense of them? Could it be your teen's way of escaping painful emotions? Could it be their attempt to keep close connections with others? What's at the root of these behaviors, and how does it fit into your teen's emotional experiences?

TOP TAKEAWAYS

The following points are key to understanding Emotion Dysregulation.

- **The Skills Breakdown Point.** Emotion Dysregulation occurs when emotions become too big to manage with current coping skills, leading individuals to focus on escaping painful emotions.
- **Mood-Dependent Behavior.** Teens overwhelmed by emotions struggle to be productive, experiencing "mood dependence" where their life revolves around removing or escaping uncomfortable emotions.
- **Rigid-Thinking Patterns.** Intense emotions can narrow focus and lead to all-or-nothing thinking, causing individuals to dismiss positive aspects and perceive the entire day as awful.
- **Poor Emotional Problem-Solvers.** Emotions surge and hinder effective problem-solving, causing individuals to disregard consequences and engage in impulsive, irrational behaviors.
- **Problems as Solutions.** Teens with Emotion Dysregulation may resort to avoidance, self-harm, or substance use to escape overwhelming emotions, often because of a belief that their emotions are too much, wrong, or unacceptable.

MOVING FORWARD AND ERADICATING THE ROOT

We made it! You've uncovered the reasons behind your teen's actions and gained a good understanding of Emotion Dysregulation. Now, let's take a step further and explore beneath the surface of these challenges. It's about facing the core issue head-on and working toward its resolution, rather than continue tending to the flames.

CHAPTER 2

‖‖‖‖‖‖‖‖‖‖‖‖‖‖‖‖‖‖

How the Fire Started

MY FIRST WEEK OF HIGH SCHOOL WAS A WEEK OF MANY firsts: my first high school dance, my first kiss, and my first in-school fight. A boy walked me home from the kickoff school-year dance and kissed me on the corner. As a new kid in a new school, I was unaware that he was someone else's boyfriend, but it wouldn't have mattered much. My low self-worth led to a steady stream of decisions that were dominated by my desperate need to be liked.

Back at school, a group of girls confronted me at the front of the cafeteria. It didn't require much to provoke me—chairs were thrown, fists flew, and kicks were exchanged. My anger always simmered just beneath the surface. When my anger wasn't directed inwardly with self-harm, it was always ready to erupt on anyone who pushed my buttons. I could transform from regulated to reactive in the blink of an eye.

The aftermath of this clash led to an inevitable suspension. This incident followed closely after I had been caught shoplifting the previous week. I barely recovered from the consequences of the last impulsive incident before enduring the next experience. My inability to return to a baseline resulted in a consistent, heightened emotional response that, when triggered, was often catastrophic or cause for crisis.

My emotions weren't just mishandled; they were an uncontrollable force, driving me toward reckless and self-destructive actions. The continuous cycle of punishment that followed failed to bring about any actual change in my behavior. A profound disconnect persisted between my emotional needs and the reactions of my environment. While people frequently criticized or punished my responses, they consistently overlooked and failed to address my underlying emotions.

Your teen's difficulties in managing emotions didn't arise overnight. They were born with emotional sensitivity, but it's their interactions with the surrounding environment that have shaped their emotional responses. This is good news for you as a parent! It means you have the ability to influence and guide their development, empowering them to improve their emotional problem-solving skills.

DECODING YOUR TEEN'S INNATE SENSITIVITY

Much like how some kids are naturally gifted in sports or arts, there are individuals who naturally possess emotional sensitivity—the Fire Feelers. If your teen is among the latter, such biological sensitivity often runs in the family; it's a genetic trait. These teens have a heightened ability to detect even the slightest emotional changes—be it a word's nuance, a facial expression, a specific tone, or a distant interaction. Because of this, they not only feel emotions more frequently, but they are also easily influenced by these subtle cues.

For Fire Feelers, emotions can be unpredictable and overwhelming. A mere dropped pencil escalates into an immediate emotional outburst, leading them to storm out of the room dramatically. Their feelings don't just surge, but they also stick around for a long time. The onset of emotions is swift and intense, and the duration is prolonged.

For example, you may disagree with your teen in the afternoon. By dinner, while you might be prepared to move on and engage in a pleasant chat, they're still caught in that emotional turbulence, unable to move forward. They might not find emotional equilibrium until the next day or even longer. When you compare an emotionally sensitive teen with their peers or perhaps their siblings, you'll notice their emotions rise faster, peak higher, and linger longer.

Advantages of emotionally sensitive individuals include a profound capacity for caring about their surroundings and the people in their lives. This heightened empathy often leads to acts of kindness toward animals and a firm commitment to activism. Many Fire Feelers channel their intense emotions into creating something brilliant and beautiful through writing, music, film, or other artistic forms of expression.

However, there's a flip side to this sensitivity: impulsivity, which also has a biological basis. For the emotionally sensitive individual, controlling impulsive behaviors becomes challenging. They often act without thinking, and this gets them into trouble.

During the late eighties, when I was in grade school, my parents, like many working-class folks of that era, wallpapered our walls. My mom prepared me for weeks, showing me swatches of what I'd see in my room, making sure it was a choice I truly liked. (I struggled with change—still do.)

But when I returned from school to a room adorned with newly wallpapered walls, my emotions consumed me. Despite my mother's efforts to prepare me, the reality of the change hit me differently. Tears formed, my throat tightened, and my stomach churned. Unable to contain my distress, I exclaimed, "It's different from what I thought. I hate it."

In an impulsive outburst, I ran to the corner of the room and tore into the new wallpaper, ripping it off.

My parents were furious. Understandably so.

If I had tolerated the distress of change—to sit with it, to ride out, and regulate without acting impulsively—the wallpaper would have remained intact. But my emotions fired up, and impulsivity took the reins, driving me to seek relief from the overwhelming feelings.

PARENT LIKE A THERAPIST

Your teen's poor ability to manage emotions developed over time. Nature and nurture played a role. This is great news because it means you can positively influence their skillfulness and help them become better emotional problem solvers.

THE INFLUENCE OF AN INVALIDATING ENVIRONMENT ON FIRE FEELERS

The behavior of Fire Feelers might appear erratic or seem like it's coming out of nowhere. Because they are so filled with emotion, their moods impede organizing behavior to achieve goals. Whether it's the challenge of attending school when overwhelming depression hits or managing a music lesson during a panic attack, their actions frequently align with their emotions rather than their aspirations. Instead of acting according to their goals and values, they often respond based on their immediate emotional urges: avoiding situations when anxious, isolating themselves when sad, or lashing out when angry.

Contributing to this emotional turbulence is an often-overlooked factor: an invalidating environment. This environment encompasses every aspect of a teen's social world that offers feedback—parents, siblings, relatives, teachers, peers, and coaches. When these influencers subtly or overtly invalidate a teen's emotions, it becomes immensely challenging for the teen to regulate themselves.

Imagine a scenario where someone is surrounded by flames, desperately shouting, "I'm not okay! These emotions are swallowing me whole. I need to escape them!" Contrast this with their caregiver, amid the same blaze, sipping coffee nonchalantly, saying, "Relax, everything's fine. Have a snack, rest a bit, or try those coping strategies from your therapist."

I met Kirsten in the behavioral health hospital where I worked, following her suicide attempt. Her story is one I've encountered many times: teens fearlessly speaking out about their ongoing sadness or depressive feelings, only to receive dismissive responses from their caregivers. Common replies like, "You're just a teenager. Mood swings are normal at your age," were all too familiar. This disregard often led these teens to take extreme measures, escalating to self-harm or substance abuse, as they desperately sought recognition for their struggles.

Kirsten's experience followed this distressing pattern. She had opened up to her mother about her persistent sadness, yet her reaction was an all-too-common line: "I was moody at your age too." This lack of understanding and validation only deepened Kirsten's sadness. The escalating cycle continued until it reached a crisis point—her suicide attempt.

This incident, unfortunately, is a regular pattern. It often takes such crises for caregivers to finally step in, unintentionally reinforcing the teen's belief that their problems are only visible, only real, when they reach a breaking point. In their minds, a dangerous narrative takes hold: "I'm only seen when I'm in crisis."

Invalidation can also present itself in well-intentioned, yet oversimplified solutions. Comments like "You're just tired, sleep it off," or "Maybe if you ate something, you'd feel better," or even "If you tackled your homework, your anxiety would ease" can inadvertently trivialize a teen's emotional turmoil. Such suggestions imply that solutions which may work for others should logically work for them. This can further exacerbate feelings of inadequacy in Fire Feelers, deepening the belief that they're somehow defective or abnormal.

When a misunderstanding between what the teen is feeling and how others respond replays over time, the sensitive individual doubts themselves: "Is my perception off? Can I trust how I feel? Is my emotional gauge malfunctioning?" They internalize a notion that they're flawed since their environment seems unfazed, implying they're defective.

This leads to situations where Fire Feelers experience discomfort when faced with powerful emotions, thinking, "Something's wrong; I shouldn't feel this way." This belief can prompt them to engage in behaviors to numb or ease the distressing sensations. When individuals encounter intense emotions in an environment that implies these emotions are excessive or easily resolved, it strengthens the idea that it is not acceptable to experience such emotions. Your teen may internalize the idea that they shouldn't feel this way and they must find a solution to make these emotions go away. Unfortunately, this pattern can lead to a cycle of self-destructive actions because the behavior provides temporary relief from the emotional intensity.

In an invalidating environment, sensitive teens receive

damaging messages that their emotional experiences are wrong. Solutions that work for other people don't work for them. This environment underestimates the significance of subtle emotions and places undue emphasis on more dramatic emotional displays, sending the message that their emotions are only valid when they reach an extreme level of intensity.

As a caregiver, your mission is to establish a firm foundation for positive behavioral change through validation. When you provide validation, you acknowledge your teen's emotional state, allowing them to stay open and curious in their interactions with you. This enables them to create mindful space for recognizing and responding to their emotions before their behaviors spiral out of control.

While you might not be responsible for your teen's innate emotional sensitivity, you can shape how they manage it. The biological basis of emotional vulnerability makes your teen predisposed to experiencing a fire of emotions. The way you tend to the dry brush will dictate how big the fire gets.

FROM INVALIDATION TO "GOOD ENOUGH" PARENTING

Let's take a moment to acknowledge and appreciate you as a caregiver. When discussing the concept of an invalidating environment, parents, myself included, may feel guilt and question if our actions played a role in our teen's struggles with emotion regulation.

I want to emphasize this: Those who may inadvertently invalidate are typically doing the best they can. They might not be aware of the power of validation or even know the techniques. That's one reason you turned to this book—to learn and understand.

It's also worth noting that some caregivers hesitate to validate out of fear. They worry that by acknowledging their teen's emotions, they're reinforcing or encouraging unwanted behaviors. Let me reassure you that validation is not the same as agreement. You can validate your teen's emotional experience without endorsing their actions. We'll cover validation—and how to do it—in Chapter 6.

You might navigate your own challenges with stress, limited resources, or a lack of support. Feeling overwhelmed naturally makes it harder to extend validation to someone else. When you're running on empty, it's challenging to offer more to others.

During one of my initial classes in grad school, where we learned psychological theories, I remember a moment of panic. My kid was just eighteen months old then. I couldn't help but voice my anxiety. I raised my hand and asked, "So, you're saying that I've messed up my kid and it's all my fault?"

The professor's response and gentle smile have since been a comforting blanket for me in this journey of parenthood.

She introduced me to psychoanalyst Donald Winnicott's theory of the "good enough mother." At its core, Winnicott's idea underscores that perfection isn't necessary in parenting. Initially, it's about adapting to the child's needs and providing an almost total environment. As the child grows, it's beneficial to introduce them to the realities of life, including moments of disappointment and not always catering to their every need. Yet, what's truly paramount is the effort to be consistently emotionally available, responsive, and to seek understanding and repair the relationship when we inevitably falter. It's not about being flawless, but being present, understanding, and committed to growth and connection.

By adopting "good enough" parenting, you acknowledge

that it's okay to have limitations. You can be loving, caring, and attentive, yet not always have all the answers. Your imperfections and occasional missteps can even be a learning opportunity for your teen, modeling that it's okay to make mistakes, and it's possible to recover and grow from them.

By being here, seeking understanding, you're showing that commitment. Trust that your child will be alright.

FINDING COMMON GROUND IN EMOTIONAL CONVERSATIONS

Your teen's struggles with emotion regulation don't arise from one isolated event. It's the culmination of repeated experiences over time, reinforcing their perception that they are inadequate or ill-equipped to handle their emotions.

Marsha Linehan's Dialectical Behavior Therapy (DBT) focuses on helping individuals manage intense emotions and improve relationships. The foundation of DBT is Biosocial Theory, which highlights how both nature (biology) and nurture (environment) shape an individual. When your teen, with their intense emotions, feels misunderstood, they might respond in ways that come across as disrespectful to you. Your reactions to these responses can perpetuate a cycle of misunderstanding and emotional distance. This ongoing cycle highlights the need for mutual understanding and validation.

The Transactional Model by Dr. Alan Fruzzetti further underscores this need by emphasizing the cyclical nature of interactions between individuals and their environment. Dr. Fruzzetti's research illustrates a pattern I frequently observed with Noah and their family.

Noah often felt overwhelmed by their emotions, yet in moments of self-awareness, they could sense their emotions escalate. Their body tensed, they felt a warmth, like their blood was boiling, and they'd experience a burst of energy. Recognizing these signs, Noah would request some time alone, saying, "I can't talk right now."

Despite these clear signals, Jill, eager to resolve the issue, would continue trying to communicate with Noah. She'd follow them, attempting to find a solution. This persistence would amplify Noah's emotions, resulting in actions like punching walls, threatening to self-harm, or leaving the house late at night.

Jill would say, "You really *do* have difficulty managing your emotions. You can't control your anger!" Such statements only solidified Noah's self-doubts and shifted the full blame of these emotional outbursts to Noah, without consideration for how Jill escalated the issue with her own behavior.

If this emotional tug-of-war sounds familiar, know that change is possible. By recognizing key concepts like emotional escalation, dysregulation, and recognizing the skills break-down point, you can manage your emotions more effectively and better support your teen. The skills breakdown point is crucial: it's when it's best to step back, validate feelings, and apply effective caregiver self-regulation strategies.

Your way of processing emotions might not align well with your teen. While a simple walk may uplift your mood, your teen may not find the same solace. This difference in biology can challenge your ability to fully grasp the depth of their emotional struggles.

Imagine waking up one day to discover your teen communicates exclusively in French, while you're fluent only in English or Spanish. Clearly, the two of you would face communication challenges. I'm willing to bet your commitment to understanding would drive you to master the French language, ensuring you could effectively ask them about their breakfast choices or remind them to clean their room.

Learning a new parenting technique is similar. By embracing the strategies in this book, you will equip yourself to handle your emotions and foster a healthier relationship with your teen.

THE GIFT AND CURSE OF EMOTIONAL SENSITIVITY

ARE YOU A FIRE FEELER TOO?

Determine if you and your teen share the Fire Feeler trait by reviewing your emotional reactions, past experiences, and learned responses with this checklist.

Emotional Reactions:

- Do sudden feelings of anger, sadness, fear, shame, or guilt often overwhelm you, even for minor reasons?
- Are your emotional reactions intense and do they last a long time?
- Do frequent mood swings or extreme sensitivity disrupt your daily life?
- Do you act on impulse, like overspending or suddenly reacting in anger?

Past Experiences:

- Were you often told your emotions, actions, or words were wrong or too much?
- Did people respond to your feelings erratically or excessively?
- Were your painful emotions and their reasons ignored or minimized?

Learned Responses:

- Do you struggle to understand or even recognize your feelings?
- Do you exhibit extreme emotional behaviors to get attention or responses from others?
- Do you often doubt whether your feelings are valid, or wonder if your reactions are appropriate?

Take a moment to reflect on your emotionally sensitive teen's traits and consider which of these qualities you may share. What strengths does emotional sensitivity contribute to your family? Conversely, what challenges does it present for both your teen and you as their caregiver? Try to recall a time you have made an invalidating remark toward your teen. Reflect on the impact this had on your interaction. As we progress, I'll encourage you to consider your thoughts, emotions, and behaviors, and the impact they have on your teen. This introspection is essential for fostering positive change and creating healthier family dynamics.

TOP TAKEAWAYS

- **Nature and Nurture:** Your teen's biologically inclined heightened emotional sensitivity can be worsened by an invalidating environment. The good news is that it's never too late to make changes in the environment.
- **The Power of Validation:** Emotions can be like a wildfire, but validation is the water that prevents them from spreading uncontrollably. By validating your teen's feelings, you create a space for them to express and regulate their emotions.
- **Sensitivity as Strength:** Your teen's emotional sensitivity is a gift, not a flaw. Nurture their empathy, creativity, and passion, guiding them to use their unique qualities to create something brilliant in their lives.
- **The Pursuit of Progress:** You don't need to be a perfect parent. Focusing on improving skillfulness and repairing harm when needed speaks volumes to your commitment to your teen's emotional well-being.
- **Rebuilding Trust:** Your consistent validation and understanding rebuild the trust your teen needs in their own emotions. Slowly, they'll learn to manage their emotional responses and rely on you for guidance and support.

STOKING THE FLAMES: YOUR ROLE IN THE FIRE

Now that you understand how the fire started, it's time to learn how your actions and reactions might unknowingly be fanning the flames. The next chapter provides insights into how, even with the best intentions, we sometimes fuel the fires we desperately seek to extinguish. Together, we'll work on understanding and quelling this blaze.

CHAPTER 3

||||||||||||||||||||||

Drop the Judgments That Fuel the Emotional Fire

WE GOT DROPPED OFF AT THE CURB. HE WATCHED AS we walked up to the door, peeking through the front window blinds. My father was always watching. We walked into the house.

I wanted to go up to my room to toss my denim duffle into the closet and turn on the TV. I just wanted to come home.

Instead, the man who had fought so hard for full custody greeted us with a confusing display of anger. The man who professed his love for us so convincingly in court, in the case that he had won.

"Stop!" he exclaimed. "Don't touch a thing. You never know who she's been sleeping with

or what she's spread around her house. Don't sit on my couch until you've taken a shower. Touch nothing. You might have AIDS."

I remember the sinking feeling in my body: stuck, frozen, standing in the middle of our living room. No words came to challenge the absurdity of his claim, only a deep, helpless confusion. Unrelenting, dysregulating, unsettling shame.

I waited, suspended in time, standing in the small front room, staring at the stairs ahead, keenly aware of his watchful eye, the weight of my overnight bag still pressing on my shoulder.

Once hidden within the safety of the bathroom, I sobbed, my face against the cool tile of the shower wall. Sadness seared through my body.

To make matters worse, his pseudo-comfort flooded me with guilt later in the day.

"I heard you crying," he said, with the sympathetic tone of a parent who beats a child and counters with, "This hurts me a lot more than it hurts you."

Only it didn't; because, upon returning home, my father's reaction immediately branded me as dirty and wrong. This internalized shame burdened me for nearly thirty years, like a denim duffel on the shoulders of a weary ten-year-old, leaving my body exhausted from bearing its weight.

Reflecting on my father's behavior, it's clear that his actions stemmed from his own struggles with the divorce. My dad hated my mom. And in seeing myself through his eyes, I hated myself too. He misdirected his pain and frustration toward me, manifesting as harsh judgments. His judgments and projections became my reality. The way you see your teen and how you convey this is critical to their self-construct.

While events and interactions can trigger emotions and influence behaviors, it's often your internal judgments about these experiences that intensify and prolong suffering. These internal judgments shape how you perceive and react to your own emotions and experiences, leading to cycles of self-criticism and difficult emotions. Similarly, external judgments, such as how you view your teen's behavior, can create conflict, misunderstandings, and emotional distance. This type of judgment can deeply impact your teen's self-esteem and how they perceive themselves. If you harbor judgments about yourself or your teen, these will get in the way of you being effective.

THE IMPACT OF JUDGMENTS: BARRIERS TO EFFECTIVE PARENTING

In our lives, various triggers can set off a chain reaction of emotions. Not only do these triggers provoke emotions, but our thoughts and judgments about these emotions can trigger even more emotional responses. We can understand this concept by looking at Primary and Secondary Emotions, where Primary Emotions connect us, while Secondary Emotions tend to create disconnection.

External events typically trigger Primary Emotions and are raw, unfiltered feelings such as joy, fear, and sadness. These emotions often lead to a sense of vulnerability, which fosters connection and closeness with others.

Primary Emotions say, "I feel sad as you grow older and need me less. While I'm incredibly proud of the person you're becoming, I'm also mourning the parts of you that are left behind. I miss the closeness we had when you were a child."

These Primary Emotions have a powerful ability to create connection, intimacy, and understanding, and to draw others toward us. However, some individuals find such raw vulnerability uncomfortable and overwhelming. Others have been avoiding their emotions for so long that these emotional thoughts don't even register. When these Primary Emotions emerge, the instinct to push them away arises. This can lead to behaviors aimed at escaping and avoiding these emotions as a protective measure.

Secondary Emotions originate from our thoughts and interpretations about our Primary Emotions. These Secondary Emotions are narrower and inflexible, making it challenging to manage or problem-solve when flooded by emotions.

Secondary Emotions bypass the underlying fear and jump straight to an act of punishment. They skip despair and head directly into criticism mode. Instead of acknowledging guilt and shame, they point fingers and lay blame. Secondary Emotions can be likened to the instinct to yell and yank your toddler when they dart into a grocery store parking lot. While it might appear as anger on the surface, what's really driving it is the intense fear of them getting hurt.

It reminds me of an interaction I had with Ryan's parent about her experience on Christmas morning. She shared that Ryan seemed indifferent about receiving his gifts, which left her feeling hurt and tempted to place blame. She noticed the urge to criticize Ryan, labeling him as ungrateful. However, she took a moment to use her skills and checked in with herself. What she was truly experiencing was grief—a mourning of the connection she once had with Ryan when he was younger. By allowing herself to feel these emotions without judgment, she could process naturally, avoiding conflict, criticism, or disconnection.

Secondary Emotions push others away. They become defenses that are the firewall that keeps the fire out so you can't get burned—but they also keep all the people out. These Secondary Emotions can lead to conflicts, misunderstandings, and more problems. It's critical that you get comfortable with your feelings because the alternative is modeling your own escape and avoidance behaviors that can also be destructive, like drinking, working too much, or having anger outbursts. Just like the old commercials from the 90s, they can learn it by watching you.

Working with Sonia proved challenging from the very beginning. Pressured speech and a bitter tone characterized her mother's phone calls. She would recount Sonia's outbursts and instances of self-harm, frequently expressing disdain and insinuating that Sonia's actions were cries for attention. Statements like, "She's always been like that. She can always get exactly what she wants. She'll fool you too. You'll see."

Engaging in these conversations often left me feeling disheartened. Sonia's mother seemed so worn down that she had given up the fight. Being a caregiver is an enormous responsibility, and it's overwhelming to juggle hope and a treatment plan aimed at ensuring someone's safety and well-being.

One question that frequently crossed my mind was, "Does she even like her child?" It was a hard question to answer.

Sonia's story is not unique. Many caregivers endure a lifetime of failed attempts to assist their teenagers, leading them to resort to blame. This can feel like a safer option than maintaining hope, given the many disappointments they've experienced. Hope can open old wounds and feel dangerous.

Judgments, whether spoken or unspoken, can shape your teen's behavior. Your teen internalizes these messages, which influence their future actions. These judgments can exacerbate challenging situations, potentially escalating them into crises. Over time, these judgments may greatly impact your teen's self-perception. Being mindful of your reactions and learning to express yourself precisely and empathetically is essential, given the lasting impact your responses can have on your teen.

TYPES OF JUDGMENTS

Let's examine some common judgments that can significantly impact the emotions and behavior of teens. These judgments often magnify the emotions surrounding an event by adding a personal interpretation that's influenced by your own life experiences rather than objective reality. This process highlights the distinction between Primary Emotions, which are the immediate, raw reactions to an event, and Secondary Emotions, which arise from the personal interpretations and judgments we layer upon those initial feelings.

LABELS

One form of judgment is the use of labels, which can act like a scarlet letter, shaping your teen's life choices. Labels like "lazy," "manipulative," "attention-seeking," or "too much" often stem from parental frustration and, once spoken, have a tendency to persist. Your teen internalizes these labels, seeing themselves through the lens you provide, and embodies the persona you've projected. The immense power of these labels carries with it a profound responsibility on your part to influence the self-talk that shapes your teen's self-esteem.

About a year ago, I attended a family gathering at my dad's place. During the event, I cracked a joke that, in my usual fashion, was off-color—sprung from my high impulsivity and the tendency to lack a verbal filter. My dad's response was typical; however, my realization surprised me. He looked at me and uttered, "You're wacky. There's something wrong with you."

This incident occurred during a phase of my life when I had reentered therapy to address some resurfacing core beliefs, one of which was the ingrained notion that "There's something wrong with me." It was a powerful realization that hit me at thirty-nine, unveiling the profound impact that a lifetime of being told that "something was wrong with me" had on my inner dialogue.

UNSPOKEN JUDGMENTS

Judgments and emotional impact can extend beyond just the words we use—they often involve our reactions too. When your teen gets emotional, a sigh or eye roll can convey the same message silently.

Fourteen-year-old Ava had been struggling with chronic anxiety for several months. Every evening, she shared her worries about school, friendships, and her future with her mother, Christine. One night, as Ava expressed her anxieties yet again, Christine, who had been supportive but was visibly fatigued from months of trying to reassure her, unintentionally sighed heavily and briefly rolled her eyes. Ava abruptly shut down, interpreting Christine's nonverbal cues as annoyance. Despite Christine's later attempts to repair harm and support her, Ava remained withdrawn. Her belief reinforced that her emotional struggles were burdensome and unworthy of attention.

When responding to your teen, consider not only what you say but how you say it. Nonverbal responses, such as a sigh or an eye roll, can significantly impact them, often carrying more weight than the words themselves. Be mindful of your tone, facial expressions, and body language. Keep in mind that your Fire Feeler has a strong sensitivity to nuances. Their interpretations are heavily influenced by their experiences and self-perception.

SHOULDS

"Shoulds" are often opinions or expectations that disregard the context and the individual. They can carry the weight of idealized images that may never come to fruition. These "shoulds" might stem from a subconscious attempt to rectify elements of your own childhood experiences. These unwritten, unspoken rules within families can sometimes lurk in the background, but when someone deviates from them, the impact can become quite loud.

In Gracie's case, her father had an inflexible "should": Gracie should get straight A's." This expectation completely disregarded the context of Gracie's battle with extreme depression and suicidal thoughts.

As a high-level professional, Gracie's dad had faced similar academic pressures during his upbringing, leading him to impose these unrealistic expectations on Gracie. The "should" served to regulate his anxiety and shield him from experiencing shame.

However, the more Gracie fell short of achieving straight A's, the more her self-worth diminished. Her father's insistence on this unrealistic expectation further exacerbated her feelings of inadequacy and depression.

Gracie internalized her father's disappointment, fostering a belief that "I should do better, but I don't, which means there's something wrong with me." Such "shoulds" create a lasting impact on both self-perception and the quality of family relationships.

PERSONALIZING

Stop looking to your teen to consider your wants, needs, and feelings, and stop assuming they're acting with you in mind at all. This leads us to the concept of personalizing, which involves assuming your teen's behavior is about you.

In my work with Evie, I often heard her parents express sentiments like, "She knows how to get to me; she's doing it on purpose to upset me." While this may occasionally hold true, it's important to acknowledge that usually your teen's actions are driven by their own emotions and impulses. Your "shoulds" and personalization assume that your teen has premeditated their behaviors when, in reality, most of the time, little to no fore-thought has gone into their actions. It's worth repeating: your teen isn't thinking about you or your reactions when they act.

I've heard the tale many times about how my husband never once offered to bring in the groceries for my in-laws. His perspective remains consistent: they never asked for help. It's easy to think your teen should have noticed you needed help and offered it but imagine me emphasizing this with a megaphone: Your teen is rarely thinking or acting with your needs or emotions in mind. And guess what? They're not supposed to.

Adolescence is a time when teenagers are quite self-focused, with a strong emphasis on their own needs and their relation-ships with peers. This self-centeredness is developmentally typical during adolescence. So, if your teen occasionally seems selfish, it's a reason to celebrate, as it means they are moving along a typical path of development.

ALL-OR-NOTHING THINKING

The concept of all-or-nothing thinking ties into the previous chapter about how our thought processes can become binary when emotions run high, leading to extreme, black-and-white perspectives.

I live with my husband and a teenager who frequently wear headphones, listening to music or podcasts. Sometimes I have moments where I feel like I'm engaging in a one-sided conversation, constantly having to reiterate my thoughts. It's a minor annoyance, but if I allow myself to think, "Nobody ever listens to me. They always have their headphones on. I'm always having to repeat myself," I'm feeding my mind with stories that I believe as facts. This intensifies my frustration with the situation. It's during these times when I might lash out or become sarcastic in my responses. These reactions stem from my judgments and all-or-nothing thinking, which can magnify the situation beyond its reality.

FRAGILIZING

Reflect on whether you might be underestimating your teen's capabilities, a subtle judgment known as fragilizing. For instance, you might presume they "can't handle" situations that are typical for their age. This could lead you to step in, such as emailing their teachers for homework exceptions, avoiding certain subjects around them, or walking on eggshells at home. Although intended to protect them, these actions pass judgment on their abilities. While assessing what your teen can or can't handle, you may also face your own fears about managing their reactions if you don't intervene to mitigate the situation. This not only limits their opportunity to develop resilience, but also mirrors your own self-judgments regarding your ability to cope with emotions.

While events and interactions are triggering and impact emotions and behaviors, it's often the judgments we have about our experience that lead to intensity and ongoing suffering. If you harbor judgments about yourself and/or your teen, these will get in the way of you being effective.

MINDFULNESS: AN IMPERFECT EFFORT IN AWARENESS

In parenting, there's a dynamic I call the Blame & Shame Continuum. At one end, there's blame: You might catch yourself thinking, "My teen isn't doing what they should. Why can't they get it together? They're always testing limits." This mindset is about blaming your teen for the difficult dynamics in your interactions.

At the opposite end lie self-judgments: Thoughts like, "What did I do to deserve this? I must have done something wrong. I'm a terrible parent." This shift toward blaming yourself or others often arises from avoiding Primary Emotions. You might grieve over your child's mental health issues or mourn the gap between the parenting life you envisioned and the reality. Resorting to blame or self-blame, which manifests as shame, is a way of evading these emotional experiences.

In this Blame & Shame Continuum, there's a parallel to your teen's tendency to engage in problematic behaviors to avoid emotions or make them go away. Recognizing this pattern is key, especially when dealing with feelings of anxiety, irritation, or sadness in your role as a parent. It's a reminder to Feel Your Feelings rather than deflect them through blame or shame.

My father alternated between blaming me for our challenges, saying things like, "You were a tough kid to parent," and blaming himself, sitting outside my bedroom, head in hands, wondering "Where did I go wrong?" Working with many parents, I've seen them struggle with these same thoughts.

In parenting, it's common to oscillate between extremes of blame and shame. However, the constructive approach involves finding a middle path—taking responsibility for your actions and helping your teen take ownership of theirs. This often requires enhancing your awareness through practicing mindfulness, as it's easy to get entangled in thoughts, emotions, and reactions and operate on autopilot, disconnected from the present moment.

When I refer to mindfulness, my aim is to encourage imperfect efforts and ease of practice. Mindfulness, in this book, means just noticing. It's about inserting a pause between your thoughts or impulses and your actions, allowing you to carefully choose your most effective next step. So, take a moment now and tune in.

THE NOTICE SKILL: OBSERVING TRIGGERS AND RESPONSES

Think about the last time your teen rolled their eyes and lashed out, perhaps calling you unpleasant names. If that hasn't happened yet, imagine how you'd feel and react if it did. What physical sensations arise? Do you feel a fiery rush of anger in your chest? An urge to retaliate and impose consequences? Or it's a lump in your throat, a desire to withdraw, and tears welling up in your eyes?

This is the essence of the Notice Skill—pausing and observing what emerges in your mind and body when you're triggered.

I once had a client whose parent, despite being well-intentioned and loving, often offered "constructive criticism." Statements like, "He's so handsome; if he would just take a shower," or "He's so smart; if he would just apply himself," were frequent. During one session, I asked the mother to share her observations about her teen while I held a crisp white piece of paper. Every time she voiced another "if he would just" comment, I folded the paper over from one corner. At the session's end, I presented the paper to her and said, "Shaina, take a look. I can see you love your son. But I want you to see the impact of your words on his self-esteem." I unfurled the folded paper, clarifying that, no matter how much I tried to flatten it again, the creases remained. They don't disappear.

The folded paper served as a striking visual metaphor, vividly illustrating how her words left lasting impressions on her son. Each fold represented another instance of her well-intentioned yet damaging comments. In this moment, the mother felt compelled to pause and truly notice the weight of her words. This led to a heightened awareness of the significant impact her language had on her teenager's sense of self-worth, empowering her with an increased ability to recognize the urge to criticize and better regulate herself.

THE NAME SKILL: LABELING EMOTIONS FOR CLARITY

Once you notice your emotions, pair that awareness with the Name Skill: the words you used to express your experience. It might sound straightforward, but when you're at a full-blown ten out of ten on the trigger scale, the gap between your experience and your actions can seem nonexistent. Yet, with practice

and patience, you can learn to notice your thoughts and emotions, label them, and respond in a more effective manner.
Remember, mindfulness isn't about achieving perfection; it's
about consciously striving to be present in each moment and
making choices that align with your values and objectives.

Imagine what could happen if you were to say, "I'm noticing that I'm getting really agitated right now. I feel the urge
to respond with anger and take away your car for a week,
but I realize that won't be productive. I'm going to take a
walk, and we can discuss this when we're both in a calmer
state." This isn't a fairy tale; such interactions are possible.
The potential outcomes are incredible. First, you're modeling
effective emotion regulation. Caregivers go first—it's the rule.
So, if you want your teen to develop these skills, you must
show deliberate practice to get them engaged.

Begin by acknowledging your own judgments. Take a
few days to observe when and where judgments arise. You'll
realize how often they sneak into your conversations. Next,
progress to clearly labeling these judgments. Use phrases such
as "I notice the thought that..." or "I'm aware of my urge to..."
This practice brings immediate judgments to your awareness,
enabling you to handle them with greater consciousness and
consideration.

Keep in mind that behaviors in your interactions with
your teen are transactional. When you refrain from getting
entangled in emotional drama, your teen doesn't experience
the emotional release that often comes with arguments. Your
choice disrupts the established pattern, empowering your teen
to manage their own emotions and behavior. This allows them
to focus on themselves without shifting blame onto you.

Be prepared for potential challenges as you disrupt the
usual pattern. We'll explore the concept of the extinction

burst soon, but it's essential to understand this: when one person breaks away from the usual pattern, others may intensify their efforts to maintain the status quo. This could manifest as more intense behaviors, heightened threats, and increased emotional expressions when you don't react in your typical manner. While safety concerns should never be ignored, you should not interpret these behaviors as a sign that you're doing something wrong.

PUTTING AWARENESS INTO PRACTICE: NAVIGATING YOUR JUDGMENTS

COMMON JUDGMENTS	EXAMPLES
Blaming the Teen	"You're such a difficult kid to deal with."
Self-Blame	"Where did I go wrong in parenting you?"
All-or-Nothing Thinking	"Nobody ever listens to me. They always ignore me."
Personalizing	"They're doing this on purpose to upset me."
Fragilizing	"I have to protect them because they can't handle this."
Labels	"You're so lazy. You should be more responsible."
Shoulds	"They should know better. I should be a better parent."

Review the table of common judgments and assess which ones you engage in regularly. Practice the Notice and Name Skill by realizing the physical sensations in your body when you have these judgments and naming the associated emotions. Keep a journal to track your progress and patterns and share your reflections with a trusted friend or therapist. Your goal is to replace these judgments with more accurate and regulated responses, creating a healthier and more understanding connection with your teen.

PUTTING NOTICE AND NAME INTO ACTION

Understanding the Notice and Name Skill is one thing, but applying it in real-life situations with your teenager is where the true transformation happens. Let's look at an example of how you can masterfully utilize these skills to navigate conflict with your teen.

Navigating Emotional Conflicts with Your Teenager
Step 1: Notice

When you're in a heated argument or a disagreement with your teenager, take a moment to pause and notice your internal state. Are your muscles tensing, is your heart racing, are you feeling defensive? Your shoulders may be tense, your jaw may be clenched, or there may be a knot in your stomach. Recognizing these signs is crucial in managing your response.

Step 2: Name

Use the Name Skill to articulate your emotions. In the heat of the moment, express your feelings calmly to your teenager. You might say, "I notice I'm becoming frustrated, and it's affecting how we're communicating. I don't want us to continue this way. Let's pause for a bit." Or "I'm noticing my own emotions welling up right now. I would like to understand what's going on, but it's challenging when we're both upset. Give me just a few minutes to breathe and then I can be there to fully support you."

By acknowledging and sharing your emotions rather than reacting to them, you model effective emotion regulation to your teenager. This approach not only helps to de-escalate the situation, but also sets the stage for a more meaningful dialogue once emotions have settled. Practice makes perfect, and as you use these skills regularly, you'll find that your parent-teen interactions become more constructive, empathetic, and connected.

TOP TAKEAWAYS

- **Awareness Is Key:** Recognize the impact of your judgments and emotions on your teen's behavior and well-being. Start by becoming more aware of your triggers and reactions to bridge the gap between emotional responses and effective parenting.
- **Embrace Primary Emotions:** Understand that Primary Emotions, triggered by events, can create vulnerability and strengthen your connection with your teen. Embracing these emotions can lead to deeper relationships and better communication.
- **Note Secondary Emotions:** Learn to identify and address Secondary Emotions that stem from thoughts and interpretations. By uncovering and addressing these patterns, you can flag judgments and better manage your reactions.
- **Watch Your Judgments:** Be mindful of the labels, reactions, and "shoulds" you apply to your teen. Your judgments can greatly influence their self-perception and behavior, so choose your words and actions carefully.
- **Shift from Blame to Mindful Responses:** Change from blame to nurturing mindful responses that promote a more composed and regulated presence.

UNLOCKING YOUR INFLUENCE: SHAPING YOUR TEEN'S INNER LANDSCAPE

Your teen's inner world is shaped by your words and actions. By refining your responses to be more effective, you gain an opportunity to uplift your teen's self-esteem and support their emotion regulation. Increasing your awareness of your judgments and shifting to a nonjudgmental perspective can improve effectiveness in your interactions with your teen. Next up, your emotions!

CHAPTER 4

Don't Let the Fire Consume *You*

AT FOURTEEN, IN THE SUMMER AFTER EIGHTH GRADE, my friend and I hopped on public transportation, and headed to hang out with boys we had met at the mall. They were older, from a town our parents dubbed "the wrong side of the tracks."

In an era before cell phones, we roamed the streets for hours, our whereabouts unknown to our parents. Meanwhile, the boys were unaware of our real story. For months, we had convinced them we were high school sophomores.

Eventually, we ended up in a house, in a room where one of the oldest boys sang along to a song and sauntered around the room. With showmanship, he sliced his arm with an X-Acto blade superficially. He laughed at the sight of his own blood in a public production.

I wordlessly watched. Curious.

At some point, my dad tracked us down. Busted into the home we landed in last. Humiliated me by sharing our real age. I was crushed. My teen brain was flooded with despair.

We drove home in silence with a shame spiral, riding shotgun. We were both fuming. I stomped to my room and slammed the door.

My spiteful impulsive part was present, and the force was strong. I turned the knob on the shower. A broken shower that would flood and leak through the kitchen ceiling. The one we were not supposed to use. *You hurt me. Now I'll hurt you.* Only the joke was on me because I was about to know real pain.

Once again, my dad busted through the door. He beat me on the bathroom floor. Cool tile against my cheek. Fetal position was my safety move...a rage rained down upon me in open-fisted blows, torrential downpour mirroring the ceiling crashing through with water below me.

When he finally left, I entered the shower, feet wet and warm from the pool of water lingering from my crime. I broke open the blue disposable razor that perched on the ledge. It was instinctual.

The pain I felt was so strong. The shame I felt was deep and dysregulating. *This will make it go away.*

The relief started a dangerous cycle.

I sat on the bathroom floor and cut my arm with the razor. A thin red line. Superficial but enough to know I had started something. A habit that saw me through several more years of pain and abuse.

I had found a way to punish myself (or maybe others). But it also brought me relief.

I'll never forget that day. Or that feeling.

Or the look in my dad's eyes when he barged in to beat me.

My dad's vulnerability was high, and his emotions had built up all day. Had he had his own regulation skills, he may have been able to respond rather than react.

LEADING BY EXAMPLE: REGULATING YOUR OWN EMOTIONS

Being prepared for your teen's behavior to trigger and test you is essential. As the adult, you must maintain emotional stability to avoid making the situation worse.

To really help your teen manage their emotions, you first have to manage your own. Your reactions can set off or reinforce your teen's behavior. So, if you want your teen to be emotionally resilient, you must model these skills yourself.

First, prepare yourself with the language and tools to control your own emotions. Understanding the structure and flow of emotions gives you practical ways to regulate them. In essence, you must understand your own emotional "brakes" before you can teach your teen how to "drive," emotionally speaking.

Knowing your emotional triggers builds self-awareness. Emotions are often triggered by external events, such as your teen rolling their eyes, talking back, or staying out late. Understanding what sets off your emotions allows you to handle your reactions more effectively. Additionally, being aware of your triggers empowers you to assist your teen in identifying their own triggers and managing their emotions. This helps them acquire the skills to regulate their emotions and behavior too.

THE PARENTAL STRESS METER: UNDERSTANDING DISTRESS LEVELS

The Parental Stress Meter provides a useful framework for understanding distress levels. Using a scale ranging from 1 to 10, it's designed to help you quantify your levels of distress. A feeling of calmness, like a spa-day scented candle, indicates low distress. Feeling overwhelmed is like encountering a five-alarm fire, signaling high distress. By being attuned to your emotional experience, you can more effectively manage your emotions. This allows you to respond rather than react, helping to prevent the escalation of emotional situations.

THE PARENTAL STRESS METER

1. **Calm and Collected:** Feeling relaxed, few signs of stress.
2. **Mild Concern:** Slightly worried but generally composed.
3. **Noticeable Unease:** Feeling uncomfortable or nervous, becoming more aware of stress.
4. **Moderate Stress:** Anxiety or distress becomes more pronounced.
5. **Agitation:** Feeling very anxious and upset, noticeably affected.
6. **High Stress:** Struggling to cope, difficulty focusing on anything else.
7. **Overwhelm:** Experiencing an intense surge of emotions; a sense of losing control.
8. **Extreme Distress:** In acute agony, the situation feels almost intolerable.
9. **Near Crisis Point:** Feeling dangerously close to a total breakdown.
10. **Absolute Breaking Point:** The situation feels completely unbearable; a crisis point.

FIVE-ALARM FIRE SKILLS: TECHNIQUES FOR IMMEDIATE COPING

Even with my experience as a teen therapist, I've faced challenges in parenting my own teenager. I've experienced teen angst, power struggles, and issues like depression and anxiety, just like you. The key difference is that I've trained myself in skills that make our interactions more effective. And still, sometimes I mess up.

Case in point: For two years, we battled inconsistent school attendance with my teen. Some weeks it would be two to four days; a full week felt like a rare win. Early on in this ordeal, I completely lost my cool. There my teen sat on the stairs—an immovable object—while I felt every nerve ending in my body blaze with tension, frustration, and helplessness.

I was aware of my emotional spiral, but it was like watching a car skid off the road in slow motion. Unable to restrain myself, I yelled, "GET UP!" My words were laced with frustration and anger. Needless to say, my outburst did nothing to resolve the situation; it just deepened our emotional tension and compounded my feelings of guilt and shame.

What I should have done—and what I've practiced since— is use my Cope & Cool Down skill. This technique helps me take a step back, assess the emotional intensity of the situation, and act rather than react, reducing the likelihood of making an already tense situation worse.

PARENT LIKE A THERAPIST

To guide your teen in managing their emotions, you must first be adept at regulating your own. If you aim for your teen to have emotional resilience, you need to embody and demonstrate these skills yourself. Keep in mind that it's a transactional process; your emotional state can trigger and reinforce your teen's behavior. How you show up emotionally sets the tone for how your teen will respond.

HOW TO COPE & COOL DOWN

Managing your teen's emotions starts with regulating your own. Follow these instructions to effectively Cope & Cool Down:

Assess Your Distress Level: Use the Parental Stress Meter to rate your emotional state on a scale of 1 to 10. If you're above a 6, consider yourself on the brink of a five-alarm fire. Take note of physical signs—for me, it's usually a rising tension in my chest and a feeling like my blood is boiling.

Step Away from the Conflict: Divert your focus by engaging in a physical activity. This could be a brisk walk, a quick shower, a brief workout, or even dancing to your favorite song. Pick something that fully engages you and helps reset your emotional state.

When the fight-or-flight response is triggered, physical movement acts as a natural stress reliever, with exercise leading to the production of endorphins—brain chemicals that function as natural painkillers and mood elevators. It helps restore the body's balance, which is often disrupted, by regulating heart rate, blood pressure, and breathing.

Paced Breathing: Inhale deeply through your nose, filling your belly with air as if you were inflating a balloon. Exhale slowly through your mouth, imagining you're blowing steam off a hot cup of coffee. Maintain this breathing pattern for three to five minutes.

Progressive Muscle Relaxation: Begin at your toes. Tense the muscles in your toes and feet for five seconds, then release. Repeat the tense-release cycle with your calves, thighs, and abdomen. Move to your hands, making fists and squeezing tightly for five seconds before releasing. Do the same with your arms, chest, and shoulders. Last, tense your facial muscles as if you're scowling, then release your jaw and eyebrows. Rotate your neck from side to side. Each time you tense, breathe in. Each time you release, breathe out. Repeat as needed.

Time It: Spend at least fifteen to twenty minutes engaged in your chosen activity, and then reassess your emotional state using the Parental Stress Meter. If your score is below 6, you may be ready to re-engage in problem-solving; otherwise, continue your chosen activity for a few more minutes. By following these steps, you'll be in a better place to effectively manage conflicts with your teen.

When emotions are running high, it's not the time to find solutions; instead, focus on coping and calming down. To reiterate: you cannot teach someone to swim while they're drowning, so avoid resolving issues when you're overwhelmed.

Using the right coping strategies has improved my family's ongoing struggles with school attendance. Yet, it remains a work in progress. When I feel the urge to yell rising, I step away. I retreat to another room, set a timer, and either scroll through social media or quietly share my frustrations with my partner. I only return to the situation when I'm emotionally prepared to be both supportive and effective in problem-solving.

This approach is challenging, but consider the alternative: Continuing dysfunctional behavior, escalating tension, and getting stuck in a cycle of helplessness and frustration. By taking a moment to Cope & Cool Down, I enhance my effectiveness and, ultimately, strengthen my relationship with my teen.

It's critical to know your own emotional "red flags," the warning signs that signal you're close to emotional overload. These could be symptoms like a racing heartbeat, tightness in your chest, or flushed cheeks. When you notice these indicators, use them as a cue to pause, step back, and breathe. Treat them as a trigger to activate your Cope & Cool Down methods.

Handling emotional situations becomes even more complex when your teen is involved. The goal is to stop the escalating, back-and-forth exchanges that can deepen conflicts. When I worked with Maria and her daughter Lizzie, the dynamic was particularly challenging. Lizzie would often antagonize her mom by throwing things, launching insults, and making threats. Essentially, she was doing everything she could to provoke Maria and keep the argument going.

To counteract this, I taught Maria specific Cope & Cool Down tactics designed to put physical distance between her and Lizzie, preventing the argument from escalating further. Maria's strategies included locking the bathroom door to take a shower, going out for a walk, or even driving around for a bit. The key was to avoid getting pulled into heated arguments. When both parties are emotionally overwhelmed, that's the worst possible time to try and resolve issues.

SIMMERING POT SKILLS: MANAGING
DAILY PARENTING STRESS

Parenting a teen with mental health issues often involves anxiety and worst-case thinking. I vividly remember the months following my own teen's depression diagnosis. One day, driving home from work, I called to check in. No answer. A sense of dread overtook me.

As I drove, my mind jumped to horrific scenarios. My heartbeat quickened and my palms got sweaty, imagining finding my child lifeless when I got home. My anxiety had tricked my brain into perceiving these fears as if they were happening in real time.

By the time I reached home, I was emotionally unraveling. I parked, raced to the door, and found my teen sitting on the couch watching YouTube, unharmed. My experience mirrors that of many parents I've counseled. To manage anxiety, they've gone to great lengths: having their teen sleep on the floor in their room, removing bedroom doors, reading text messages, even scouring diaries.

Simmering pot behaviors lead to moderate distress. These situations typically fall between a 4 and 6 on the Parental Stress Meter. They're the "everyday crises" that build up over time, making you dread what's next but still allowing you to carry on with your life. It's a draining existence.

Yet, the dread I felt in the car wasn't entirely baseless. My child has experienced depression and suicidal thoughts. This constant worry affected my daily life, and once kept me in a perpetual fight-or-flight mode, always bracing for the worst.

The catch is that our persistent state of anxiety—despite our vigilance and repeated checks—isn't helping our children. What really works is learning self-regulation to enable co-regulation. To provide a stable environment for your teen, you need to maintain a calm and non-anxious presence. That's the most impactful way to support them emotionally.

This is when the Feel Your Feelings skill becomes vital for managing emotions effectively. This technique teaches you to be present with your emotions without trying to change them. Instead of suppressing or impulsively reacting to your feelings, you learn to navigate through them, trusting they will eventually pass—and they do.

Emotions typically last between sixty to ninety seconds when allowed to unfold naturally. It's our ongoing thoughts, judgments, and interpretations that extend their duration.

To make room for new emotional states, you have to pass through your current ones. This involves being present with your emotions, observing what surfaces, and giving it space without attempting to alter it. While this process can be painful, it's the most effective pathway to emotional healing.

By fully acknowledging your emotions, you enable them to dissipate, paving the way for new emotional experiences and growth.

LET'S PRACTICE THE FEEL YOUR FEELINGS SKILL

Identify the Emotion: First, tune into your body. What is the emotion physically feeling like? Is it tension in your shoulders, a pit in your stomach, or perhaps a burning sensation in your chest?

Track Its Movement: Observe how the emotion moves through your body. Breathe deeply into these sensations. Feel the emotion rise and fall like waves.

Observe Without Judgment: Maintain focus on the emotion without altering it or assessing its validity. If your thoughts wander, redirect your attention back to your physical sensations. You're building on your Notice Skill here!

Use a Body Map: When I work with clients, we often use a body map to depict these feelings. I provide an outline of a human figure—like a gingerbread man—and invite them to color, scribble, or draw to show where and how the emotion manifests in their body. This helps to deepen your connection to what you're feeling.

Describe the Emotion: After fully experiencing the emotion, take a moment to put it into words. This is your Name Skill in action! Use descriptive language to convey how it feels, and if possible, imagine images that could represent this emotion. This helps you to detach the emotion from any triggering thoughts or events and gives you another layer of understanding.

Remember, It's Temporary: Trust that emotions are transient; they come and go. Understanding that the emotion will eventually pass helps you manage the moment more effectively.

By following these steps, you're not only acknowledging your emotions but also allowing them to move through you, reducing their Intensity over time. This approach will not be easy, but it's effective for emotional management.

SCENTED CANDLE SKILLS: SELF-CARE AND PREVENTION STRATEGIES

For managing emotions, your vulnerabilities represent the daily stressors that accumulate, typically ranking within the one to three range on the parental stress meter. Consistently neglecting these stressors can lead to a buildup of tension, making you more susceptible to being pushed over the edge by a challenging day with your teen.

To counter this, proactive Self-Care strategies play a pivotal role. The goal is to maintain a state of relative calm and balance. Engaging in Self-Care practices equips you to handle life's unpredictabilities more effectively. Here are some strategies to consider:

PRACTICE DAILY MEDITATION

Signal to your body that it's time to meditate. Drop your shoulders. Unclench your jaw. Soften your eyebrows. Close your eyes. Notice the way your body makes contact with your seat. Feel your feet connected to the floor. Begin to focus on your breath and notice how your chest rises and falls with each inhale and exhale.

Breathe out slowly and exhale all the stale air within your body. Then, breathe in through your nose and as you do so, lift both arms out to the sides in a T. Feel your heart open as you stretch out to the sides like you're about to give a big hug to a loved one. Exhale slowly through your mouth.

Inhale through your nose again and stretch your arms up to the sky. Reach for the sun and feel the tension in your shoulders. If you'd like, hold each wrist, and gently pull to feel a nice stretch down the side of your body.

With an intentional exhale, slowly lower your arms. Let them hang and let gravity do its job. Sit with yourself for a few natural breaths. You may notice thoughts enter your mind and that's ok. Don't attach to them or push them away. Just let them flow through.

With a final deep breath, inhale through your nose for a count of four. Hold the breath at the top for a count of seven. Exhale through your mouth with a "whoosh" for an eight count. Open your eyes and return to the present.

KEEP A GRATITUDE JOURNAL

Gratitude is a powerful mindfulness practice. Get yourself a notebook and keep it by your bed or in your desk drawer. At the end of each day, write down three things that you are grateful for that day. But don't just write them. Write three to five sentences under each list item that describe *why* you're grateful. As you break it down, allow yourself to feel this in your body. Connect the sensations. Practice feeling your feelings in pleasant ways.

One way this practice has been really helpful for me is with finding silver linings. Even though my teen has depression, I'm grateful that I have professional connections to get prompt care. I'm grateful that I'm self-employed so my schedule is flexible to attend to the unpredictable. This is not intended to dismiss, invalidate or minimize your difficult experiences. Think of it as putting training wheels on the bike you can't ride yet. It's helping to keep you upright when the road is rocky.

PROTECT YOUR SLEEP

Prioritize your sleep and aim for a full seven to nine hours. Sleep deprivation has a direct impact on your brain and, consequently, your ability to manage your emotions. Your amygdala, a walnut-shaped region in your brain responsible for regulating emotions, doesn't function properly without adequate sleep. This can lead to a lowered mood and heightened responsiveness to triggers, meaning you're more easily provoked. Your emotional reactions can escalate quickly, making you feel crankier and far from your best self, which is not conducive to effective parenting.

Work backward and apply the +1 rule. If your goal is to wake up at 6:00 a.m. and get a full eight hours of sleep, plan to be asleep by 10:00 p.m. Allocate an extra hour for winding down and aim to be in bed by 9:00 p.m. This provides you with some leisure time to scroll your phone, listen to a podcast, or unwind. Afterward, you can peacefully transition to sleep. If you encounter racing thoughts or find it hard to relax, consider trying body scan meditations. It's highly likely that you'll drift off to sleep before the audio ends.

NOURISH YOUR BODY WITH FOOD AND MOVEMENT

To maintain an optimal ability to manage your emotions and remain a stable force for your teen, you need to nourish yourself. Eat a morning meal high in protein. This raises your brain's tyrosine levels and helps your brain produce neu-rotransmitters called norepinephrine and dopamine, which give you energy and make you feel awake and alert.

When you're in a high stress experience, your body enters fight or flight. Without movement, your cortisol (the stress hormone) rises, your health is impacted, and chronic stress stays with you. When you intentionally move your body you "complete" the flight and expend the energy that your body's chemistry built up for you. Aim for at least twenty minutes of movement per day to your mobility level.

NURTURE SOCIAL RELATIONSHIPS AND HOBBIES THAT BRING JOY

It can feel almost impossible to focus on yourself when your teen is struggling. For many parents this thought induces guilt or shame, or their own mood dependent behavior gets in the way.

During our intake interviews with parents to join our parenting program, many express that their lives are cen-tered around work, worry, and parenting. While it's entirely understandable that your teen's struggles can consume your thoughts and energy, this constant focus on them is not helpful. Taking time for yourself is essential to recharge and rediscover your identity beyond the role of a caregiver. And the line that "once they are ok I'll focus on me" won't fly. Your child needs you to prioritize Self-Care now, so you can be the best version of yourself and provide the support they truly need.

SELF-CARE STRATEGIES IN ACTION

For Self-Care, the key is to establish a sense of consistency and take tangible, actionable steps. This involves setting clear, achievable goals and seamlessly integrating them into your daily routine to ensure they become habitual. Schedule these activities in your calendar and make it happen!

IDENTIFY YOUR ANCHORS

Identify routine activities that ground you—these are everyday tasks that help you stay anchored in the present moment. These activities should be simple and already a part of your daily life. One of my anchors is cooking dinner. With my favorite nineties rock music playing in my ears, a candle flickering, and the flow of following a recipe, I'm fully engaged and present in the moment.

STRENGTHEN YOUR CONNECTIONS

Connect with those who uplift and support you. Dedicate moments for shared experiences, like a walk with a friend or a recurring date night. Acknowledge your innate need for connection and foster it—it's essential.

BUILD A STRONG EMOTIONAL FOUNDATION

Recognize and proactively address any vulnerabilities that could potentially trigger reactive emotional responses. Vulnerabilities refer to aspects of your life where you may have neglected your own well-being, such as inadequate sleep, high levels of work-related stress, or insufficient social support.

If my dad had implemented a plan to manage vulnerabilities or developed skills to deal with triggers, maybe he wouldn't have acted in ways that didn't align with his values, ways that brought more conflict and drove us apart.

We might have had the chance to work together to problem solve and find a way back, rather than landing in a place filled with abuse and self-harm. It's now clear to me, as a parent myself, the significance of recognizing and addressing our vulnerabilities as a crucial aspect of Self-Care. That day, my father was overwhelmed by a cascade of emotions, feeling vulnerable, scared, and uneasy. When everything piled up, his frustration and anger spilled out uncontrollably. His reactions were the direct result of unmanaged stress and emotional triggers.

TOP TAKEAWAYS

- **Lead by Example:** As an adult, your emotional stability sets the tone for your teen's behavior. Model effective emotion regulation to guide them through challenging situations.
- **Practice Self-Care:** Prioritize your well-being with Self-Care strategies like meditation, gratitude journaling, sleep, and maintaining social connections to handle stress and stay resilient.
- **Cope & Cool Down:** Use the Cope & Cool Down skill to manage emotions. Identify distress levels, engage in physical activities, and practice relaxation techniques for better emotional control.
- **Feel Your Feelings:** Master the "Feel Your Feelings" skill to sit with and process emotions. This technique encourages you to actively engage with your feelings, allowing you to experience and acknowledge them rather than ignore or suppress them.
- **Build Strong Foundations:** Manage your own vulnerabilities to prevent emotion-driven behaviors. By taking care of yourself, you provide a stable base from which to guide and nurture your teenager's emotional well-being.

TENDING THE SLOW BURN:
GRIEVING WHAT NEVER WAS

Now that you recognize the importance of managing emotions in the moment, it's time to go deeper. There's likely a persistent "slow burn" you need to address—mourning the loss of what never materialized or what can never be. The upcoming chapter sheds light on this nuanced form of grief. Together, we'll journey through understanding and healing this lingering pain.

CHAPTER 5

〰〰〰〰〰〰〰〰

Watching the Building Burn

IN OCTOBER 2012, MY MEMBERSHIP IN MY OWN FAMILY expired.

I warmly greeted my grandmother at my cousin's wedding, an event that occurred mere days after I had delivered my own save-the-dates.

But in return, I got a stone-cold stare and the turn of her cheek away from me.

She didn't say a word. Her actions left me confused, anxious, standing there staring at a full globe of big white hair, a grown woman refusing to look me in the eyes.

I called her the next day. Though I was shaking, I was determined to remain calm. Gentle. Neutral.

"I can't help but notice that you ignored me at the wedding. Have I upset you?"

The emotional labor required to wade through the toxic communication channels within my family was exhausting. And yet I always swam harder than anyone to keep my place in the pool.

Her response was cold and crisp, but calm.

"After everything I've done for you, I take it as a personal affront that you'd invite your mother to your wedding. I can't continue to be hurt by you like this. You are no longer welcome in this family."

And so it was.

No holiday gatherings.

No birthday cards.

Not a single call or text.

From anyone.

I had spent a lifetime fawning to fit into a family that I believed didn't want me.

And in the end, they really didn't.

Sometimes, life unfolds differently than we expected. The emotions, reactions, and choices of others result in a lack of control over the vision we once held. Sometimes, we yearn for closeness or connection, but our loved one doesn't reciprocate our needs.

Grieving and acknowledging that I would never have the family I had hoped for was a crucial step toward moving forward. Your life with your teen may differ significantly from your initial vision for them, but acceptance marks the beginning of finding harmony in that reality.

TRUE ACCEPTANCE AND GRIEVING THE VISION

True acceptance involves embracing the reality of the life you have, while also allowing yourself to grieve the vision you once had. I've come to realize that this process of acceptance and grieving is a shared experience for parents of teens.

As children transition from dependency and close connection to becoming autonomous individuals who sometimes behave in perplexing and even maddening ways, it can be challenging. You go from having a little one snugly wrapped around your neck, clinging to you, to suddenly watching them detach. They start making their own choices and exploring various paths, which can make them seem like entirely different beings.

This shift can be disorienting. You feel a sense of pride as you witness your child growing and gaining independence, but you also experience a profound loss as they move further away from the person you once knew, someone you've influenced, someone you've raised.

They inch closer to a version of themselves that, at times, feels like a stranger. Occasionally, they may even seem like someone you don't want to know anymore. It can lead you to question your own identity as you adapt and change to meet the needs and demands of this new individual. This person, once a reflection of you, now challenges you, provokes you, and brings waves of anxiety about the uncertainties you never even knew were possible.

And then there's the grief. Oh, the grief. It cuts deep into your soul and burns like a raging fire inside you.

When my own child began experiencing mental health issues as a teenager, grief reared its head, but this time as the Blame & Shame Continuum. Initially, it manifested as blame. I was angry and frustrated, and I remember those moments of judgment. "Why can't you just go to school?" "You're not using your coping skills." I was infuriated, trapped in anger and blame, and it wasn't benefiting either of us.

At times, that blame transformed into shame. *Was this my fault? Was I not present enough? Was this some form of karma?* I convinced myself I deserved this, and I questioned my abilities as a teen therapist, unable to help my own child. However, lurking beneath both blame and shame, a deep sadness consumed me, along with a profound grief, and the realization that the life I had envisioned was lost. I had looked forward to having a teenager, given my connection with this age group, but the reality didn't align for me. Instead, it felt like every day was a struggle, and I grieved the daily loss of the life I had expected.

This grief is not discussed enough. While we talk about teenagers being moody and testing limits, we overlook the pain that we, as parents, experience. The moment we realize our child has become someone we no longer recognize is something we don't usually discuss, and then we find ourselves having to become someone new as well.

It's not just our teenagers seeking a new identity; it's us needing to redefine who we are and what our reality is. *This isn't the life I had imagined. It's not what I pictured. But it's the life I have now.*

THE UNSPOKEN PAIN OF PARENTING

Within you, there are parts filled with love and adoration for your child. There are parts that will fiercely protect them no matter what. And there are parts that are grieving, wishing for a different path, longing for life to be less challenging.

One of the most impactful exercises we engage parents in during group sessions is a mindful observation of a photograph of their teenager as a baby. This practice encourages them to deeply connect with the pain, loss, and grieving process that unfolds as they navigate the challenges of parenting a teenager.

Let's do a similar exercise right now. Begin by signaling to your body that you're about to engage in a meditative moment. Place your hands palm up on your lap, relax your jaw, lower your eyebrows, and let your shoulders drop. Inhale slowly and deeply through your nose, holding the breath for three seconds, then release it slowly through your mouth as if exhaling through a straw.

Take a moment to gaze at a photo of your baby. Observe the expression on their tiny face. Pay attention to the emotions that well up within you. Initially, you might feel joy, love, and nostalgia. However, it's likely that feelings of pain and loss will also emerge. Allow these emotions to surface. Breathe into the sensations within your body without trying to push them away. Make room for your grief because it's real. Your teenager is no longer that baby in so many ways, yet in some respects, they still are.

Now, reflect on your vision for your baby's future. No parent envisions the struggles of the teenage years. No parent expects their baby growing up to experience depression or self-harm. When you cradle your newborn, thoughts of navigating mental health challenges later in life rarely cross your mind. This reality is a deviation from the idealized vision.

Feel the disappointment that accompanies this realization. Make room for that disappointment without judging yourself. Acknowledge the thoughts you believe you can't express aloud. Remember that countless parents before you have felt the same disappointment you're feeling now. It's a normal part of the journey. Allow it to come and go. It doesn't define your worth as a parent; it's a testament to your humanity.

Place your hand on your heart. Inhale and exhale, noticing the rise and fall of your hand against your chest. Take a moment to appreciate yourself for being present here and now, for showing up for yourself today. You're doing the best you can. The tools in this book will assist you in doing even better, and each new day presents fresh opportunities to try again.

RADICAL ACCEPTANCE AND GRIEF

Radical Acceptance, a term introduced by Marsha Linehan in the context of Dialectical Behavior Therapy (DBT), entails refraining from fighting reality when things do not align with your desires. It involves letting go of the anger and frustration that might keep you trapped in a cycle of suffering, choosing instead to embrace what is, rather than what you wish it to be.

For me, this process is truly and completely a grieving process. Remember, in order to address your emotions, you must allow yourself to Feel Your Feelings. Radical Acceptance begins with recognizing that your life or circumstances do not match your ideal vision. It acknowledges that there might be no practical means to problem-solve or change the situation. The essence of this practice is coming to terms with an unalterable reality.

Revisit the vision you held for your child. Where do you sense the pain? What aspects do you wish were different? Observe how your body responds and the tension that might arise within you. Pay attention to your facial expressions. You may notice signs of internal conflict when you recognize sadness, grief or frustration co-mingling with love and gratitude. Acknowledge this inner turmoil. Take a deep breath, allowing your belly to expand as you inhale. Exhale slowly through your mouth. Let your face relax into a slight, Mona Lisa-like smile—an expression that signals acceptance to your mind.

Now, shift your focus toward acceptance. See your current situation with clarity. Acknowledge the profound pain and sorrow that accompanies it. Breathe slowly and deeply as you stay connected to these emotions inside your body. Allow yourself to experience these feelings without self-judgment. The pain is undeniably real but embracing it can open up opportunities for progress. Continuing to resist and battle against it only keeps you stuck in suffering.

Radical Acceptance is not a one-time event. It's like training a puppy to sit—repeated practice is required. Just like the puppy might jump up, run around, and resist your commands, you'll find your mind drifting away from acceptance. It's your responsibility to gently guide your thoughts back to acceptance, again and again.

PARENT LIKE A THERAPIST

True acceptance means grieving the vision of your life as you had hoped it and accepting the version of your life as you have it.

The process of Radical Acceptance often unfolds as a lifelong journey, triggered by various life circumstances. In my case, having more children was not in the cards for me, and every time I reflect on this, a deep-seated grief wells up within me.

My pregnancy at the age of twenty-six came as a surprise. I was living at home, just two months after graduating from college with a 3.86 GPA, despite battling a dangerous drug habit. I was functional, but I was fooling myself. There were no celebrations, no partners with plans, and no joyful ultrasounds shared with family. Instead, there was fear, shame, and secrecy. However, my pregnancy ultimately served as a catalyst for change. It helped me realize that the world was bigger than the pain within me, and I cleaned up my act, becoming the parent my child deserved.

As the years passed, I yearned to become a parent again, to share more love and laughter with a chorus of children at home. Unfortunately, having more kids was not to be. I grieved in waves, with tears streaming down my face as I passed by playgrounds. My body seemed to scream at me that time was slipping away, while reality hammered me with the truth—I was meant to be the parent of an only child.

I sought new ways to create community, to surround myself with love, laughter, and a life of purpose. Yet, I couldn't escape the fact that I never experienced the milestones most people envision when planning for a child.

My body holds this loss, and there's a space in my heart that will never be filled. I lead a fulfilling and happy life, filled with gratitude. Often, I think to myself, *If I could only have one child, at least I got the best one.* I don't feel that something is missing; it's not. But I do acknowledge that the vision I once had for my life is different, and when I remember, the grief resurfaces. I sit with it, make space for it, and then I continue. That, to me, is Radical Acceptance.

Linda, mother to her sixteen-year-old daughter, Emily, experienced a similar process of coming to terms with her grief through Radical Acceptance. Linda had always envisioned a close-knit family where she and her daughter shared everything, from engaging in crafts and hobbies to confiding their innermost thoughts and secrets. But as Emily entered her teenage years, their once effortless connection began to fray. Linda found herself struggling to accept both Emily's worsening depression and her choice of friends, who appeared to be making questionable decisions.

One evening, after a heated argument with Emily about her choice of friends and her declining school performance, Linda decided to apply the principles of Radical Acceptance that she had been learning. She retreated to her room, intentionally setting aside space and time to process her emotions. Here, she confronted her own expectations and the heartache she experienced for the close mother-daughter bond she had longed for.

After calming herself, Linda approached Emily with a different perspective. Instead of pushing her own agenda or trying to change her daughter, she asked open-ended questions, genuinely seeking to understand Emily's point of view. Linda chose to accept the reality of who her daughter was becoming, especially recognizing that Emily was grappling with depression and was not the happy-go-lucky daughter she once had.

Over the next few weeks, Linda continued to practice Radical Acceptance. She joined a parent group, where she found empathy and validation from others facing similar challenges. This helped her cope with her feelings and allowed her to be more present for Emily without the burden of her unmet expectations.

Accepting your family for who they are provides you with the freedom to choose how you want to define your relationship with them. It brings peace and allows you to stop trying to change them or expecting them to be something they can never be. It grants all of you the space to breathe.

SEEKING SUPPORT AND COMMUNITY

Your grief, sadness, and loss are entirely valid and real, but they should not become your teen's burden to bear. Your teen is experiencing their own emotion regulation challenges. Expecting them to hold it all together so that you don't fall apart is an unfair demand. Your teen is not responsible for managing your guilt, shame, grief, and disappointment by changing their behavior. This is why Seeking Support is of utmost importance.

Imagine a target with your teen at the center—the bullseye. They reach out for support from their outer circles. You, as the parent, are the next concentric circle outward, providing support to them. When you seek support, it's critical to look outward, beyond your circle, and not burden your teen with the responsibility of being your support system, sounding board, or confidant.

Seeking Support offers you a sense of community and the validation that you are not alone in your struggles. It helps you shed shame, which might compel you to conceal your challenges, and connects you with others who normalize the process. This, in turn, enables you to be your best self at home by relieving the stress you carry. By Seeking Support, you can empty your stress cup and engage with others through open and honest expression of your Primary Emotions.

Be mindful of what you're taking ownership of and what you might unknowingly be placing on your teen to "fix." I recall a day after my parents announced their divorce when I sought solace in my room. As I lay on the floor next to my bed, crying, my dad entered my room a few minutes later and sobbed while lying on my bed. He told me he didn't want the divorce either. Strangely, I didn't feel comforted. It didn't feel like a shared experience. Instead, it seemed like his emotions were something I needed to attend to. There didn't seem to be space for my own emotional response. This marked the beginning of years where I felt like the grabber people used to reach cans on the top shelf at the grocery store. I wasn't granted permission to be autonomous; I was treated as an extension of my father, serving to fulfill his emotional needs.

Radical Acceptance is indeed a grieving process. It involves learning to accept your teen for who they are and relinquishing the vision of who you wanted them to be. When you establish your own support network to navigate this loss for yourself, you create an opportunity to build a relationship with your teen based on acceptance of who they truly are. Acknowledging the fire in your life allows you to devise a plan to extinguish it and rebuild.

CREATE YOUR CIRCLE & PRACTICE SEEKING SUPPORT

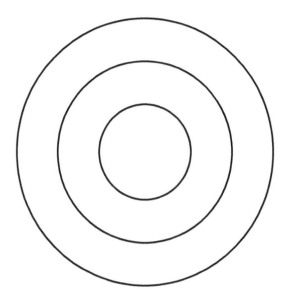

As you work toward Radical Acceptance, Seeking Support can be transformative. It helps you build a firm foundation of understanding and compassion, both for yourself and your teen. Take some time to create your Circle of Support, envisioning it as a target with your teen at the center.

STEP 1: ACKNOWLEDGE YOUR
TEEN AT THE BULLSEYE

In the center of your metaphorical target, visualize your teenager. This represents your teen's needs and challenges at the heart of your family's dynamics.

STEP 2: RECOGNIZE YOUR ROLE
IN THE NEXT CIRCLE

Move to the next concentric circle around your teen. In this circle, see yourself as the parent, caregiver, or guardian. This is your role in supporting your teen.

STEP 3: IDENTIFY YOUR OUTER
CIRCLES OF SUPPORT

Now, imagine additional concentric circles radiating outward from the center. These outer circles symbolize various sources of support beyond your immediate family. Consider the following sources of support:

- **Friends and Peers:** Think about friends who have experienced similar situations or who can lend a listening ear and emotional support.
- **Support Groups:** Seek local or online support groups for parents who are experiencing similar challenges. These groups provide a space to share experiences, gain insights, and find encouragement.
- **Professionals:** Explore therapy or counseling options for yourself. A therapist can help you navigate your own emotions, provide guidance, and offer tools for effective communication with your teen.

- **Extended Family:** Reach out to extended family members who can offer support, understanding, and sometimes even respite care.
- **Educational Resources:** Consider reading books, attending workshops, or enrolling in parenting classes focused on understanding and assisting teens with mental health concerns.

STEP 4: BUILD YOUR CIRCLE

Now, reach out proactively to individuals or resources that can form the various rings of your support circle. This step is about creating a network of support tailored to your unique needs and circumstances.

STEP 5: COMMUNICATE AND CONNECT

Once you've identified your support network, don't hesitate to communicate your needs and challenges openly. Share your experiences, thoughts, and emotions with those who are a part of your circle. This open dialogue fosters understanding and compassion.

TOP TAKEAWAYS

- **Embrace the Journey:** Acceptance means letting go of the life you envisioned and embracing the unique journey your teen is on.
- **Grief is Valid:** Acknowledge and honor the grief that comes with the gap between expectations and reality.
- **Seek External Support:** Reach out to a supportive community to share your journey and unburden your teen from being your sole support.
- **Release Unrealistic Demands:** Your teen is not responsible for easing your grief; focus on your own healing and support network.
- **Cultivate Authentic Connections:** By practicing Radical Acceptance, you create space for genuine relationships based on who your teen truly is.

SHIFTING YOUR PARENTING PERSPECTIVE

Pause for a moment and release the urge to mold your teenager into something they're not. You've started addressing your own inner challenges, so now it's time to redirect your energy toward understanding and supporting your teen. This change in focus will allow you to build a more empathetic and constructive connection with them as you both work toward positive behavioral changes at home.

CHAPTER 6

⁝⁝⁝⁝⁝⁝⁝⁝⁝⁝⁝⁝⁝⁝⁝⁝

Extinguish the Flames with Validation

AUNT "TT" HAD ALWAYS BEEN MY ALLY IN MY FAMILY. As a teen, I'd spend weekends at her home, a welcome escape from the tension and trouble of my own.

We'd sit amidst the Marlboro merchandise, and she'd always make me laugh. I recall the felt sensation of her papasan chair and the mingling scents of cigarettes and perfume. In a family that often felt like struggle, she was a safe haven.

We'd dance to the Grateful Dead, exchanging books and stories. We'd discuss boys as we smoked on the front porch. She treated me like a human during a time when my family environment felt dehumanizing.

Only later in life did I realize I was attracted to her uniqueness as a black sheep. Smart, messy, and impulsive, she was the adult embodiment of my wounded world. Her presence was a gift; a mirror reflecting a sense of normalcy. She was the key to my sense of belonging.

However, when my grandmother turned her back on me, Aunt "TT" wasted no time in stirring the pot within the family.

I confronted her. "I know you're talking about me. Why?"

I can't recall her reason, but I remember my own plea: "I thought you, more than anyone, would understand what it's like to not belong." Her response was anything but validating; she denied my experiences, saying that I deserved to be ostracized for my choices.

The one person who had previously understood and normalized my experience suddenly turned against me. It was a devastating blow, especially since she had been the one who made me feel seen and like I belonged. Validation is an incredibly potent tool, and without it, your teen may suffer more and find it even more challenging to make positive changes.

VALIDATION BEFORE CHANGE

When you validate your teen's feelings, you acknowledge their emotions and experiences without judgment, using words and phrases that express understanding and acknowledgment, such as, "I can see that you're feeling frustrated right now," or "It sounds like you had a tough day." This acknowledgment helps your teenager feel heard, understood, and respected, even if you don't necessarily agree with their viewpoint or behavior. It also provides them with the starting script for how to Notice and Name their emotions, the foundation for self-regulation.

When your teenager feels validated, they are more likely to accept your input or requests. This means that your teenager is willing to consider your perspective or engage in problem-solving, knowing that their emotions have been acknowledged and respected. Acceptance must precede problem-solving if you want to influence positive change at home.

On the other side, invalidation occurs when we, whether intentionally or unintentionally, through words or actions, convey that emotions don't make sense. This might involve statements like, "They're overreacting. You're trying to manipulate. This isn't important. I can dismiss this easily. It's not worth my time, respect, or interest." Even if you don't consciously think these things, this might be the message the other person receives through your actions or tone.

You might have reservations about using validation because you worry it could be interpreted as condoning undesirable behavior or fear that acknowledging feelings might exacerbate the situation. This concern was very real in Harper and her mother Nicole's story. Nicole could clearly see the sadness in Harper's eyes, the sense of isolation, and the tearfulness. However, she was hesitant to address it or mention the thin red lines on Harper's wrist out of fear that it might intensify Harper's emotional distress. Nicole worried that by naming it, she might inadvertently push Harper further into depression or even give her the idea of self-harm or suicide.

However, the opposite is the case. Validation is the first step to effectively managing intense emotions. It conveys to someone that their feelings are valid and understandable in a given situation. Validation doesn't imply agreement. You can validate your teen's emotions without endorsing their behavior. Understanding why your teen wants to stay out until 3:00 a.m., even if you don't allow it or agree with it, is validation. It means comprehending their perspective and the reasons behind their actions. It harkens back to Chapter 1 when we discussed the function of emotions—now we're taking that knowledge and applying it to our interactions with our teens.

For instance, you can understand that deep depression and intense emotional distress might lead to thoughts of escape or even suicidal ideation. You don't like it, it's frightening, and you certainly don't condone it, but showing your teen that you understand their perspective is important.

Validation is a tool for enhancing relationships. It can defuse conflicts by acknowledging the kernel of truth in their concerns. Validation signifies that you're attentive, empathetic, and nonjudgmental. It conveys your commitment to the relationship—even when you disagree—without resorting to conflict. In the context of your relationship with your teen, it's possible to hold differing opinions without descending into discord or hostility.

EXAMPLES OF INVALIDATION AND VALIDATION

Invalidation includes statements like, "You're overreacting. Don't be so sensitive. It was just a joke. You're too emotional right now, calm down. Think positively. You're so negative."

Invalidation can also manifest as "one-upping," where someone tries to diminish your teen's feelings by saying their own experience was worse. For example, if your teen says their boyfriend broke up with them at a football game, and someone responds with, "You think that's bad? My boyfriend broke up with me through a text." This type of response feels very invalidating.

On the validating side, responses include phrases like, "You're making sense. Your feelings are important. It's okay to feel upset, and I'm here to listen." A simple and effective validating response might be, "That's really tough. I can see it's hard for you."

Validation does not involve fixing your teen's problems.

Validation can be challenging because we're inclined to be problem solvers, but our teens with intense emotions may struggle with this. If we constantly step in to solve their emotional problems, they won't have the chance to develop this skill for themselves. Instead, validation is about creating a space where your teen can sit with their emotions, learn to tolerate them, and feel empowered to decide how to navigate them and eventually make changes on their own.

Feelings themselves are not dangerous or bad; it's often the behaviors that result from these feelings that we try to suppress. We don't want to reinforce impulses that attempt to make the emotion disappear. Your aim is to assist your teen in expanding their capacity to tolerate their emotions through validation.

I hope that you'll practice these concepts in real-life situations. It might require some trial and error, and it might feel awkward initially. Don't be discouraged if your teen gives you a puzzled look or a negative response when you try one approach. Learning this new way of communicating is like learning a new language. It may feel strange at first, but that doesn't mean it's not effective.

Numerous methods exist to show validation. It's worth noting that any one approach may not work for everyone. Try different methods of validation until you find the right mix of tools that work best for your family.

BE PRESENT VALIDATION

The cornerstone of validation lies in your attentiveness. In my days as a play therapist, we had a saying: "Your attention flows where your nose goes." It means that when your teen is trying to communicate something, take a moment to pause whatever you're doing, whether it's cooking dinner or watching TV, and give them your focus. During a conversation, set aside distractions like your phone, and make eye contact. When you can convey to your teen that you're truly listening, that what they say matters, and that they have your complete attention, it encourages them to approach you with important matters.

Admittedly, being present isn't always easy, especially amidst the demands of daily life. My spouse and I employ an accountability buddy system to stay on track with this. We give each other a gentle nudge when we notice the other person half-listening while scrolling through their phone. Your validation won't be perfect every time, and that's fine because you're aiming to be a "good enough" parent—like the research supports! Seek support to help you stay committed to this valuable practice.

REPEAT-BACK VALIDATION

Repeat-Back Validation involves providing an accurate reflection of what your teen has expressed by paraphrasing or echoing back what you've heard from them. Instead of saying the exact same words or using a condescending sing-song tone, you're selecting words that convey "I heard you, and I understand. Your feelings make sense."

For example, if your teen shares their irritation about a peer not contributing to a school group project, you might respond by saying, "That's really frustrating." In this way, you acknowledge your teen's annoyance and mirror their experience, confirming that you've heard them and empathizing with their feelings.

MIRROR VALIDATION

Mirror Validation involves interpreting nonverbal cues. It's essentially about reading your teen's mind using your long-standing knowledge of their body language, tone, and facial expressions. In those moments when your teen arrives home, and you notice their shoulders tensed up to their ears, with clenched fists, and you ask, "What's wrong?" while they respond with, "Nothing, I'm fine, I'm fine," you know that they're not fine because their words don't align with their body language.

In such moments, you can say, "You're saying you're fine, but I can see that you're really tense right now. Your tone suggests you might be upset. It seems like something may have happened at school that upset you." It doesn't necessarily mean you have to talk about the issue or ask more questions about it. Acknowledge their feelings without the immediate pressure of finding a solution or discussing the situation further.

TIMELINE VALIDATION

Timeline Validation revolves around acknowledging your teen's past learning experiences. This validation method is something you've been preparing for your whole life! You possess an intimate knowledge of your teen's life story, the sequence of events they've gone through, and this equips you perfectly to say things like, "It makes perfect sense that you'd feel sad and rejected when Tony didn't talk to you at lunch today, given your history of bullying and rejection from others." Or you might express, "I truly understand why you wouldn't want to go to the dog park, considering your past experience of being attacked by a dog when you were six."

Take a moment to conduct a timeline scan. Ask yourself why your teen's current emotions make sense in light of their history. This approach communicates to your teen that you truly see and understand them, that their feelings are valid based on what's already happened in their life.

HUMAN STRUGGLE VALIDATION

Human Struggle Validation involves recognizing the common human experience, and it can be particularly impactful for Fire Feelers who often doubt or question their own emotional responses.

During the pandemic, when high schools canceled proms and graduations, our team devoted countless hours to acknowledging and normalizing the widespread sadness and loneliness felt by teens. Through Human Struggle Validation, we communicate that many individuals face similar challenges, thereby making their emotions more relatable and understandable.

This approach is not to be mistaken for an invalidating response, where you might dismiss their feelings with a statement like, "Everyone's upset right now," which implies "You're fine." This is counterproductive.

The power of this form of validation lies in understanding your teen's biological sensitivity, as discussed in Chapter 2. Your teen may have come to believe that something is wrong with them due to the intensity of their emotions, thinking, "My emotions are overwhelming, and I can't trust my own feelings. There's something inherently wrong with me." By normalizing their experience, you're telling them, "It's entirely understandable to feel this way right now, and many others are experiencing similar emotions." This transformation in perception helps them feel heard and understood, and reduces their belief that something is inherently wrong with them because of their emotions.

BE-REAL VALIDATION

The last type of validation is all about being your authentic self! In this context, you step out of the typical parent-teen dynamic and connect on a human-to-human level with your teen. You show them that you genuinely care about them as a person and can respond to them without the parental facade, just for this moment. It's about saying things like, "It's really tough that you didn't get into Princeton," or "I'm genuinely upset that Declan didn't invite you to hang out with the rest of the guys."

Being real means you can display your emotions with your teen, not in a way that centers the situation on yourself, but in a way that lets them know you can empathize and be authentic with them. This reaffirms that you validate their experience, that you listen to them, and that you genuinely see them. It creates a space where you can engage with them as equals in the conversation, allowing them to be their true selves too.

Resist the urge to fix your teen's problems. You can ask them, "Do you want me to help you solve this, or do you just want me to listen?" Practice leaning back in your chair, even sitting on your hands if necessary. Keep in mind the Seeking Support skill, with your teen at the center, and avoid conveying the message that they need to be okay for you to be okay. The goal is to help them develop the resilience to cope with their emotions rather than removing those emotions entirely.

Validation makes the brain more flexible and opens your teen to the possibility of considering your perspective and requests. Acceptance must precede problem-solving if you want to influence positive change at home.

VALIDATION STEP-BY-STEP
STEP 1: ACTIVELY LISTEN

When engaging in validation, the first step is active listening. Maintain eye contact and remain engaged with your teen. Be conscious of both your verbal and nonverbal cues. Approach your teen with genuine curiosity and interest, paying attention to your facial expressions, eye rolls, and reflexive reactions. My husband often talks about professional wrestling, which he's passionate about. He wants to share a story about it, and sometimes, I find myself sighing, rolling my eyes, or even picking up my phone during his storytelling. While I am technically hearing the words he's saying and occasionally responding, my nonverbal cues and reactions fail to convey that what he's saying matters to me. (Truthfully, it's not important to me at all.) However, with your teen, when they share something meaningful, it's critical to avoid diminishing its importance with your own facial expressions, tone of voice, or automatic reactions, some of which you might not even be aware of until they're pointed out. Therefore, mindfulness and awareness are key. You want your teen to feel comfortable coming to you and sharing their thoughts and feelings. This is your chance to reinforce that openness.

STEP 2: NOTICE AND NAME

In the second step of validation, pay close attention to what your teen is feeling at that moment and choose a word that accurately describes that emotion. Take a guess if necessary, for instance, saying, "You seem really sad." Even if your guess turns out to be incorrect, it's okay because almost every teen appreciates the effort, and they won't hesitate to correct you. Making an attempt is far better than staying silent, which might give your teen the impression that you're not interested in understanding them.

STEP 3: USE VALIDATION SENTENCE STARTERS

Here are some sentence starters to help you get started with validation:

- "I understand where you're coming from…"
- "Your feelings make sense…"
- "It's okay to be upset…"
- "You're not alone in feeling this way…"
- "I'm listening…"
- "That sounds really tough…"
- "I can see this is hard for you…"
- "That sucks…"

These are just starting points to begin the conversation. Be open to any adjustments or clarifications from your teen during your discussion. This not only shows your willingness to listen but also helps you gain more insight into their unique experience and feelings.

You can also validate through your actions. For example, listen attentively, offer a tissue if they're crying, or provide a hug if it seems appropriate. Validation doesn't always have to be verbal. It could also be something like, "You seem really down right now; let's go for a drive and get some soft-serve." This approach shows that you understand your teen's feelings and care about their emotions, allowing them to sit with those feelings without pressure to discuss them.

No matter whether you validate through words or nonverbally, the most important thing is that you reflect back the emotion without judgment. The objective is to convey that you comprehend how they feel, without attempting to solve their problem. Let them know that you understand them, that you're right there with them in their emotional state, and that's where validation ends. It's about showing tolerance and recognizing that their thoughts, feelings, or actions make sense, even if you don't agree with them or approve of the situation. This requires having self-regulation skills to prevent immediate reactions like anger, fear, or frustration. You need these skills to help your teen manage their own emotions effectively.

STEP 4: PRACTICE

I've found that achieving genuine validation in my relationship with my teen was a gradual process that required time and patience. What became clear was that nonverbal validation held more effectiveness for us. My teen primarily prefers validation through actions rather than words. It involves gestures like bringing them a cold drink when they feel overwhelmed or covering them with a blanket when they are anxious. This form of validation eliminates the potential for misinterpretation, especially when parenting a Fire Feeler teen who is acutely attuned to subtle shifts in tone. It allows them to feel truly seen and supported in their emotional experience. Validation remains an ongoing process of trial and error, so be patient with yourself as you discover what works best within your unique relationship with your teen.

As you practice validation, look for opportunities to understand your teen's point of view. Consider what makes sense about their behavior and how you can communicate this understanding. Review the various types of validation discussed in this chapter and identify which ones feel most authentic to you. Create scripts and practice them, even recording yourself to assess how they sound. Plan ahead for how you will respond if your teen doesn't react with immediate kindness and gratitude. Change takes time, and your success in validating is not solely dependent on your teen's response.

Validation is crucial for building collaborative change with your teen's cooperation. It equips them with the skills to regulate their emotions, enabling you both to work together on problem-solving. Validation helps calm emotional flames and makes the fire manageable, allowing you to contain it with precision.

TOP TAKEAWAYS

- **Validation Before Problem-Solving:** Remember, validation paves the way for problem-solving. Validating your teen's feelings builds a foundation for your teen's ability to Notice and Name their own feelings and to be felt, heard, and understood by you.
- **Empathy, Not Agreement:** Validation doesn't mean agreement. You can understand without condoning, creating space for authentic conversations with your teen.
- **Power of Normalizing:** Acknowledge that emotions are part of the human experience. Normalizing their feelings reduces the sense of isolation and self-blame.
- **Vary Your Validation:** Use different validation techniques—from mirroring to history in context—to tailor your responses to your teen's unique emotional landscape.
- **Stay Consistent and Patient:** Building validation skills takes time. Consistency is key. Stay patient and committed to practicing this foundational step in supporting your teen's emotion regulation skills.

FROM ACCEPTANCE TO CHANGE

Recognition and acceptance of another's emotions and experiences is the foundation for healing. When someone can acknowledge your pain and sit with you during your difficult moments, it creates a profound connection and opens the door to coping and making positive changes. Conversely, the absence of validation intensifies pain and loneliness, ultimately deepening the emotional abyss.

Now that you've taken steps to acknowledge your own judgments and emotions, and your teen has felt seen and heard as well, you're both in a position to move toward positive change. In the next section, we'll cover strategies for problem-solving and influencing behaviors to foster harmony in your home.

CHAPTER 7

‖‖‖‖‖‖‖‖‖‖‖‖‖‖‖‖‖

Okay, the Fire's Out. Now What?

MY HIGH SCHOOL BOYFRIEND WAS AWARE OF MY STRUG-gles with self-harm, and he knew about the strained relationship I had with my dad. Each night, we'd spend hours on the phone, sharing secrets and disclosing our deepest feelings, hopes, and dreams. I trusted him and the consistency of his emotions. He treated me with the sensitivity that a single dad couldn't provide to me.

One night I cut too deep. I scared myself. Or maybe I didn't. Maybe I just wanted the intoxicating response of someone who cares so much it almost feels like too much. It feels like a drug.

A phone call and twenty minutes of travel time and he was at my door, rubbing alcohol and dressing in hand. He sat on the stoop with me and cleaned my wounds. The warm burn of alcohol seeping into my skin burned like hell, but that was just part of the ritual. Part of the pain that settled my shame. It was the same warm feeling washing over my body that later

I'd experience with drinking alcohol—your insides warming under a fuzzy blanket next to a cozy fire.

At school, others would notice my cuts too. I could feel their gaze fixated on the fading marks on my arms, or they would discreetly slide up a sleeve to reveal their own. They saw my pain. They saw me. And the behavior became a racing stripe that led to creating a community of others whose mere existence could validate my experience. I didn't need words to show them how much it hurt. They knew.

When my dad found out, he took me to a therapist. At least then he knew too. At least he could see it on the outside.

The self-harm I engaged in provided short-term relief, but the caring and connection that followed were intoxicating. While many people tend to focus on the triggers for such behaviors, it's the internal and external consequences of these behaviors that offer the most insight into why we engage in them. By recognizing the secondary gains of self-destructive actions, we can gain insight into how to reduce the negative aspects and enhance the positive ones.

To understand this topic, let's explore the basics of behaviorism. Every behavior has a purpose and is motivated by underlying factors. By becoming skilled at pinpointing the core reasons behind your teen's actions, you can gain a better understanding of how to promote more preferred behaviors.

DEFINING BEHAVIORS

A behavior is anything you can see your teen doing—from their eye rolls to the way they slump on the couch. Even their tone of voice when they answer your questions counts. You may notice a depressed teen isolating in their room, making self-critical comments, or tearing up at certain topics. These are all behaviors.

A trigger is something that sets off a behavior. It could be external, like a sarcastic comment from a sibling, or internal, like a worrying thought. Keep in mind that behaviors are transactional. You and your loved ones can trigger one another. Imagine your teen receiving a text from a friend saying, "I hate you." That text becomes their trigger, and they respond by screaming loudly and making self-harming threats. Subsequently, their behavior becomes your trigger, prompting you to rush into the room to assess the situation. We continually trigger each other, and our behaviors are constantly influenced by these interactions.

Consequences happen right after a behavior. They're the natural results of actions. The feeling of relief after avoiding a stressful situation can encourage your teen to keep avoiding it. Or the comfort of eating junk food can make it a hard habit to break. The soreness from a new exercise routine might discourage you from sticking with it. In short, what happens immediately after a behavior helps us understand why it keeps happening or why it stops.

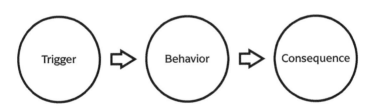

In this sequence, a trigger initiates a behavior, which in turn results in a consequence. The consequence that occurs within seconds of the behavior is what ultimately helps us understand the purpose or function of that behavior.

IDENTIFYING TARGETS: CHOOSING WHAT YOU WANT TO CHANGE

In choosing which behavior to address first, safety is always the top priority. Life-threatening issues like self-harm must be addressed before anything else. We're not going to talk about socks on the floor in a messy room when your teen is self-harming. Then, look at behaviors that are causing the most stress or taking up a lot of time. If long arguments are a regular occurrence, that's a behavior to prioritize.

To change a behavior, first clearly define what you want to change. Be specific. For example, if you want your teen to hand in assignments on time, don't say, "Stop procrastinating." Instead, say, "Start your homework right after school at the kitchen table." This clear instruction makes it easier to understand and follow. When working on behavior change with your teen, use precise and specific language.

First, and I can't stress this enough, *choose one* behavior to target for change. Define the exact actions that make up the behavior. Identify the specific circumstance and environment that trigger the behavior. Make it so clear that if I ran a mental movie, I could picture the full scene in my head and reenact it.

USING DIFFERENT BEHAVIOR MANAGEMENT TECHNIQUES FOR TEENS

DIFFERENT is your comprehensive behavior management system, neatly packaged in a memorable acronym. It serves as a reminder that when you want to witness change in your teen's behavior, it all begins with you. As always, parents lead the way, and by embracing the DIFFERENT approach, you'll be firmly rooted in the science of behavior change while confidently supporting your teen.

The acronym for behavior management is "DIFFERENT":

- **D**uration
- **I**ntensity
- **F**requency
- **F**eed the Meter
- **E**scape the Pain
- **R**emove Reinforcers
- **E**xtinction Planning
- **N**atural Consequences
- **T**each Positive Opposites

Let's break down the elements of DIFFERENT:

DIF sets a baseline for the behavior, providing you with a starting point to assess whether the subsequent strategies are effective. This involves measuring the behavior's "Duration," observing how long your teen engages in it, monitoring its "Intensity," and tracking its "Frequency" in your teen's routine.

FE provides methods to boost positive behaviors by associating them with positive responses. "Feed the Meter" involves encouraging and rewarding behaviors to increase their occurrence, while "Escape the Pain" focuses on alleviating discomfort to reduce undesirable behaviors.

REN offers approaches to diminish problematic behaviors by either removing the inherent rewards or allowing Natural Consequences to unfold. "Remove Reinforcers" involves identifying and eliminating factors unintentionally reinforcing unwanted behaviors. "Extinction Planning" acknowledges an initial increase in the behavior when attempting to stop it and emphasizes the importance of consistency in your response. "Natural Consequences" allow your teen to experience the direct results of their actions, promoting learning from their choices.

Last, **T** underscores the importance of teaching skills to replace the behaviors you aim to decrease. "Teach Positive Opposites" encourages the substitution of undesirable behaviors with positive, constructive alternatives.

Now, let's explore how to apply each of these interventions effectively.

DURATION

Once you've pinpointed a behavior you want to change, the next step involves reducing the time dedicated to it. For example, if you and your teen frequently find yourselves immersed in lengthy arguments, work on decreasing the Duration of these arguments by using your Cope & Cool Down skill. As you become more skilled at disengaging and self-regulating, you'll actively shorten the time spent in conflict with your teen. Furthermore, keeping track of the time allows you to step back and adopt the role of a mindful and scientific observer of the situation. This perspective removes you from being deeply entrenched in the moment and provides you with a measurable metric for improvement.

INTENSITY

If you find yourself frequently resorting to yelling and making threats out of frustration, the goal should be to gradually decrease the Intensity of these reactions by incrementally improving your coping strategies. Start by reducing the volume and tone of your voice during moments of frustration. Instead of yelling loudly, express your concerns calmly in words. As you become more skilled at managing your reactions, work on shifting the language you use from threats to constructive communication. A plan that goes from one hundred to zero abruptly isn't practical or effective, but a gradual reduction in intensity over time can be a realistic goal.

FREQUENCY

The more a behavior is repeated, the more firmly it becomes ingrained in the routine, making it progressively harder to break the cycle. One approach to address Frequency is to track the behavior over time. Keep a record of when the behavior occurs and how often it happens. This tracking can help you identify patterns and triggers that may contribute to the behavior. Once you have a better understanding of the Frequency and patterns associated with the behavior, you can then begin the work of reducing its occurrence.

Parents of Fire Feelers sometimes succumb to all-or-nothing thoughts like "This doesn't work" because of the slow rate of change in these teens. Having baseline metrics not only helps measure progress but also generates hope. Small signs of progress pave the way for significant changes over time. However, they require you to employ all of your skills to navigate the often challenging middle phase before reaching your desired outcome.

FEED THE METER

Think of Feed the Meter, or Positive Reinforcement, as a way to boost healthy habits in your teen. It's about giving them verbal affirmations, a pat on the back or a little reward when they do something you want to see more of. This positive reinforcement makes it more likely that you'll see these behaviors continue.

If your teen has been actively working on improving their

relationship with a sibling and responding to conflicts with increased patience and kindness, be sure to offer immediate acknowledgment when you witness them effectively handling a disagreement calmly. You could say, "I noticed how you kept your cool during that discussion. I'm so impressed with the skills you're using!" This kind of positive feedback can serve as a significant motivator for your teen.

Practical Ways to Reinforce Your Teen

Praise Specific Actions: If your teen finishes their homework, let them know you're proud. Say something like, "I saw you worked really hard on your project today. Great job on staying focused."

Small Rewards: These don't have to be big. Maybe your teen has been keeping their room clean. Surprise them with their favorite snack or an extra hour of screen time as a "thank you."

Physical Affection: Sometimes, a high five, a pat on the back, or a hug (with their permission) can say more than words. It's a way to show that you appreciate them.

Celebrate Effort, Not Just Results: Say your teen studied a lot but didn't get the grade they hoped for. Instead of focusing on the score, praise their effort: "You put in a lot of time studying, and that's what really counts. I'm proud of how dedicated you are." The goal is to encourage the behavior, not just the result. This approach builds their confidence and keeps them motivated to try their best.

Create a Shaping Plan

Behavior change often needs to be broken down into smaller, manageable steps. Consider driving a car; for example, you don't just hop in and drive immediately. You begin by learning the rules of the road and understanding the mechanics like shifting gears and pressing the accelerator. You master how these components work together, reinforcing proficiency in each step along the way.

Shaping is a method that breaks down complex behavior changes into manageable steps. This approach involves deconstructing a behavior into smaller components and reinforcing each one as it is mastered, thereby increasing the likelihood of achieving the ultimate goal. Back to our example, learning to drive a car can be divided into individual skills such as steering, braking, and staying in the lane. Reinforcing each step as it is learned helps in developing the overall skill of driving. By reinforcing one step at a time, you progress toward the full behavior, enhancing the chances of success.

In our parent group, we use the example of cleaning a messy room to illustrate the concept of shaping. When confronted with an extremely cluttered room, tackling everything at once can feel overwhelming. However, breaking the task into smaller steps, such as starting by gathering all the laundry into a hamper, then addressing the trash, and finally organizing the papers into piles, makes it more manageable. You're essentially doing the same work but in a way that creates smaller victories, which add up to a sense of achievement.

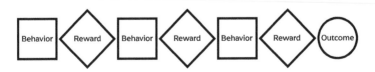

Create a Shaping Plan that focuses on achieving the ultimate behavior as the end goal but breaks it down into smaller, manageable steps. For example, if your goal is for your teen to consistently attend school, start with a weekly target of getting out of bed and brushing their teeth. Reward this initial step and be patient, understanding that they may not attend school immediately. In the next phase, the milestone could be getting dressed and coming to the kitchen on time for breakfast. This incremental approach helps prevent conflicts that can arise from setting overly ambitious goals and allows your teen to feel accomplished one step at a time. Remember to utilize your self-regulation skills here: Cope & Cool Down and Seek Support. Change takes time, and although you can't accelerate it, you can approach it with skill and patience.

To reinforce effectively, focus on all behaviors that move your teen toward the desired goal behavior, and do so as quickly as possible after the behavior has occurred. This will help your teen to clearly understand which behaviors are being reinforced. Timing is critical when reinforcing desired behavior. Consider a baseball coach providing feedback to a player practicing their swing. If the coach waited until after twenty swings to say, "Nice job," the player wouldn't know which swing was actually good. However, if the coach reinforced the player's successful swing with immediate feedback, the player would better understand what they did right and how to improve. To maximize the effectiveness of reinforcement, time it as closely as possible to the desired behavior, or even during the behavior itself. This ensures that the reinforcement offers clear and concise information to promote the desired behavior in the future.

ESCAPE THE PAIN

Escape the Pain, or Negative Reinforcement, occurs when a behavior increases because it helps avoid discomfort. A teen who yells to relieve tension and feels less anxious afterward is an example of negative reinforcement. Another example is taking Tylenol to relieve a headache; the relief reinforces the action of taking Tylenol. Because of the immediate relief they provide, these strategies can potentially perpetuate harmful behaviors, as is often the case with self-harm.

Self-harm can ease intense emotions such as loneliness, shame, and hopelessness quickly, increasing the likelihood of the individual engaging in this behavior again as a coping mechanism. Breaking the cycle of self-harm can be challenging because it operates as a negative reinforcer. When a person experiences overwhelming emotions, self-harm can offer a temporary escape from that emotional distress. Over time, positive reinforcement may come in the form of social understanding or validation, further complicating efforts to break the behavior. This combination of negative and positive reinforcement creates a complex cycle that can be difficult to overcome. Self-harm is a challenging behavior to address because there are few coping strategies that can alleviate emotional pain as quickly.

Anna, a seventeen-year-old, had been struggling with self-harm for almost a year. At first, she found that it briefly eased her feelings of loneliness and isolation. When overwhelmed, self-harm provided a quick, albeit temporary, escape from her emotional pain.

Self-harm brought Anna immediate relief, reinforcing the behavior as a coping mechanism for intense emotions. She received positive reinforcement through online communities that empathized with her struggle, further complicating her ability to break this cycle. This blend of negative and positive reinforcements ingrained it as a deeply rooted behavior.

Concerned about Anna's worsening signs of depression, her parents approached her with compassion, eventually discovering her self-harm habit. Seeking professional help, they worked with a therapist who introduced Anna to alternative coping methods. One effective technique was the "face in ice water" method, where Anna would plunge her face into a bowl of ice water during moments of intense emotional distress. Using cold water calmed her body down and decreased her heart rate, acting as an immediate physical counter to her overwhelming feelings, similar to the immediate relief she sought through self-harm.

After using the ice water technique, Anna's parents consistently provided positive reinforcement. They praised her for choosing to communicate her urges and for using the new coping strategy. This positive attention and encouragement from her parents were pivotal in reinforcing these healthier behaviors. They spent quality time together, like going for dog walks or watching her favorite movies, reinforcing her choice to communicate rather than self-harm.

Over time, Anna relied less on self-harm. She found the ice water method effective for immediate relief and felt more comfortable discussing her feelings with her family. Gradually, with the support of her therapist and the positive reinforcement from her parents, Anna developed healthier ways to cope with her emotions, leading to significant progress.

To replace problem behaviors with healthier skills, the new behaviors must serve the same function and intensity as the target behavior. Substituting self-harm with something unrelated, like eating a cupcake, is not an effective solution because it serves a different purpose. Seeking positive reinforcement through sweets provides a different outcome than escaping the pain of sadness or shame. Replacement behaviors that address the underlying tension, such as engaging in intense exercise or seeking social interaction are more effective for decreasing painful emotions. When supporting teens who engage in problematic behaviors like self-harm, suicidal ideation, running away, or skipping class, be strategic and find ways to address the function of the behavior without reinforcing it.

As a parent, you can apply Escape the Pain reinforcement effectively. For instance, if your teen has had an exceptional day or accomplished something significant, you might take over one of their regular chores, like doing the dishes, as a reward. This action shows them their efforts are noticed and appreciated by removing the "pain" of the chore.

Understanding Teen Behavior: It's Science, Not Manipulation

What might look like manipulation in your teen's actions is based on a scientific understanding of behavior. Remember to drop the automatic judgments to be effective! Both you and your teen play a role in shaping and maintaining behaviors.

For example, if your teen shouts to get what they want, and you give in by handing over the car keys, you're reinforcing their shouting. They learn that this behavior works. (So why *wouldn't* they keep doing it?) On your end, you might find that giving them the car keys stops the shouting, bringing you some peace, helping you Escape the Pain. This becomes a cycle where their behavior and your response to it reinforce each other.

All behavior makes sense. All behavior has a cause. Learn how to find the root function of your teen's behaviors and what to do to see more of the behaviors that you want.

REMOVE REINFORCERS

It's important to spot and change things around your teen that might unintentionally encourage the behaviors you're trying to reduce. Sometimes, without meaning to, parents can make a behavior worse by giving extra love and attention, or giving in to what their teen wants after the behavior occurs. Removing the accidental reinforcers is a process called Extinction.

When teens skip school, consider what comforts at home might unknowingly contribute to this behavior. A comfortable bed, easy access to their phone, television, or even having food delivered can inadvertently create a more enticing home environment compared to attending school.

Of course, you will still want to identify the root cause of their avoidance (remember that behaviors are their way of solving problems), but you also want to be mindful of additional reinforcers that may further solidify the behavior. On days when your teen skips school, make the home atmosphere less appealing. Limit their access to phones and television during school hours and avoid excessive accommodation of their needs. By implementing these measures, you're removing the home comforts that could potentially strengthen their decision to skip school.

When a reinforced behavior no longer receives reinforcement, it often diminishes. Using extinction, such as planned ignoring, can reduce behaviors once maintained by attention.

This technique should only apply to safe situations, never to dangerous ones. For example, ignoring a teen's name-calling or persistent demands can be effective, as long as it is done with consistency.

Consider implementing planned ignoring when your teen challenges family rules. Start by addressing the behavior once, and then purposely redirect your attention elsewhere. Let's say your teen keeps asking to order food delivery despite your prior response that dinner will be ready in an hour, and the answer is no. Instead of allowing this to escalate into an argument, calmly respond the second time they ask, saying something like, "I've already explained dinner is in an hour, and today is not a day for delivery. I will not answer this again since I don't want it to become an argument between us." This approach involves removing your attention while maintaining respect and responsiveness toward your teen. This change in repeated responses, which was previously reinforcing for your teen, can contribute to a reduction in your teen's incessant asking.

Expect your teen to follow you and persist in their behavior, even though you are taking a different path. If needed, remove yourself from the environment by taking a shower, going for a walk, or driving around the neighborhood. With consistent removal of reinforcement, this pattern will shift, but this will take time.

I've worked with many families where parents require coaching to block and ignore behaviors rather than feed into them and fuel the fire. As your teen intensifies, you will naturally want to respond or give in.

Lilith was a fifteen-year-old female who came to me following treatment in a residential program. She would yell and threaten her parents if she could not get her own way.

Lilith's frustration would often escalate to physical outbursts. She would scream at them and deliberately knock items off shelves, further intensifying the tension and helplessness her parents experienced.

I collaborated with Lilith's parents, teaching them the importance of blocking and ignoring certain behaviors instead of inadvertently reinforcing them. Breaking the cycle of reacting and giving in was challenging and demanded immense self-discipline. Lilith's parents would have to retreat to the basement and practice ignoring the onslaught of insults and objects.

Over time, Lilith's parents slowly learned to resist the urge to engage with her when she lashed out. Instead of providing the fuel that her fire craved, they learned to remain calm, unruffled, and unwavering in their expectations. They set clear boundaries and communicated their love and support while refusing to engage in power struggles. They fostered an environment where they valued her thoughts and emotions, yet her explosive tactics were no longer effective.

Be sure to reinforce other positive and adaptive behaviors as substitutes for the targeted behavior and keep in mind that when reinforcement is removed, your teen may initially attempt to increase the behavior to regain the reinforcement. However, with consistent non-reinforcement, the behavior will eventually diminish.

EXTINCTION BURST PLANNING

When you change rules or responses, your teen might have a powerful reaction. This is called an "extinction burst." For example, if you tell your toddler "No" to a candy bar in the store and they cry louder or throw a tantrum, that's an extinction burst. Or, if you set new rules for your teenager, they might get more upset or argue more than usual.

During an extinction burst, teens will try harder to get what they want. Their brain tricks them into believing that by being persistent, they'll get the same result as before. This can be a tough time for parents, but it's crucial to stick to your decision and not give in. If you stay firm, eventually these behaviors will lessen and stop.

If things get worse before they get better, it doesn't mean you're failing. It's a sign that the changes are taking effect. This is often the point where it's tempting to give up and go back to old ways, but that will just start the cycle over.

To help you through this, focus on using your Cope & Cool Down skill and Seeking Support. Keep consistent with your new rules. Over time, your teen will see that their old ways of reacting don't work anymore and will adopt better habits.

When you try to stop a behavior that has been rewarded for a longer period of time and more frequently, the reaction will be stronger. Stay firm and don't give in, because giving in can make the behavior even stronger and harder to stop later on. Think of it like a slot machine in a casino: if you win once, you're more likely to keep playing to win again. The same goes for behavior—if it gets rewarded, it continues. So, be strong and consistent with your approach.

Being inconsistent with rules or consequences can make things worse, causing confusion and more testing of limits. Parents need to be clear and steady with their rules and the consequences of breaking them. This helps create a stable and secure environment for your teen.

When you want to address and change one of your teen's behaviors, it's essential to engage in a constructive conversation with them first and establish an Extinction Cope Ahead

Plan. Instead of changing your responses without prior communication, take the time to inform them about your intentions and the reasons behind them. When discussing the behavior in question, use a calm, clear, and nonjudgmental tone. For example, you can say, "I've noticed you spend about six hours alone in your room each day (Duration), and it seems like you're feeling more down lately (Intensity) than usual. You've also come to me twice this week (Frequency) after hurting yourself."

Then, explain the new way you're going to respond. Tell them you're doing this because you care and want to help them find better ways to cope. Make sure they know you're not punishing them, but supporting their growth.

For instance, you might say, "From now on, when you tell me you're feeling the urge to harm yourself, I'll come and sit with you, and we can watch *The Office* together (Feed the Meter). I'll also help you use the coping strategies you learned with your therapist (Escape the Pain). But, I won't have deep talks with you in your room right after you've harmed yourself. We can talk before that happens, but doing it after might teach your brain that deep talks are a bonus after self-harming (Remove Reinforcers)."

Don't expect your teen to be grateful! When implementing behavior management techniques, prepare yourself to expect unpleasant responses from your teen. These can include indifference, arguments, rejection, emotional blackmail, and even aggressive behavior. Continue to validate your teen's feelings and stay the course in your approach, even when faced with these challenging reactions. Avoid getting into arguments or debates; instead, maintain a calm and consistent response. Over time, your teen will understand the new expectations and boundaries you have set, and the unwanted behaviors will decrease.

Create an Extinction Cope Ahead Plan

EXTINCTION COPE AHEAD PLAN

To create your plan, follow these prompts:

1. Describe the specific behavior you want your teen to change.
2. Reflect on how your own actions may inadvertently reinforce this behavior.
3. Identify the alternative actions you will take instead.
4. Write a script for discussing these changes with your teen, emphasizing care, compassion, and clear communication.
5. Anticipate how your teen may react to these changes, and plan your Cope & Cool Down strategies for when these reactions occur.
6. Recognize the red flags that your behaviors are approaching crisis levels, and establish a plan for addressing these red flags.
7. Outline how you will reinforce signs of progress, and provide positive reinforcement to your teen.
8. List Self-Care activities that support your well-being during this difficult time.
9. Identify individuals in your Seeking Support circle who can provide assistance and guidance.

Creating an Extinction Cope Ahead Plan is a proactive way to prepare for potential challenges that may arise during the extinction process. To accomplish this, carefully consider how you will handle and address your teen's potential reactions and behaviors during this time—how will you respond when they escalate? When will you cope, and when is it a crisis? Use the Parental Stress Meter to gauge your own reactions and know when to take action.

Reinforcing progress by praising and rewarding your teen, as well as spending time together to discuss their achievements, can help motivate and encourage them. Remember to take care of yourself during this process by maintaining a support system and seeking encouragement and validation. Extinction is a gradual process, and it won't happen overnight, but with commitment and consistency in your approach, you will see progress.

NATURAL CONSEQUENCES

Natural Consequences are a great way for teens to learn from their own actions. When they see the direct results of what they do, it helps them understand their choices better. For example, if your teen doesn't study for a test and then gets a bad grade, that's a natural consequence. It shows them the importance of studying and may encourage them to study more next time. Another example is if they stay up late watching TV and then feel tired the next day. This tiredness directly results from staying up late.

It's beneficial to your teen's development to let these Natural Consequences happen. Don't step in to fix everything for them. Let them experience these safe, everyday consequences to help them learn and grow. It teaches your teen to think about their actions. However, make sure these consequences are safe and not harmful.

Understanding the Right Use of Punishment

Punishment involves applying a negative consequence to deter or reduce a specific behavior, such as time-outs or the withdrawal of privileges, like phone use or going out with friends. It shows that certain actions lead to unwanted results.

Keep punishments short, not lasting over twenty-four hours, and ensure they pertain to the behavior. For example, if your teen sneaks out at night, not letting them go out the next night is an appropriate consequence. This approach aims to encourage them to consider the consequences of their actions without being overly punitive.

Punishment often produces short-term behavior changes but can lead to emotions such as anger or resentment. Overusing punishment may even cause your teen to distance themselves from you. Excessive punishment can harm your relationship by eroding trust and respect. Keep punishments brief and relevant to promote learning without damaging your bond.

Relying excessively on punishment can establish a cycle of fear, where your teen avoids certain actions to avoid punitive consequences rather than understanding why those behaviors are problematic. Instead, emphasize positive reinforcement and teach your teen healthier behaviors to replace problematic ones.

When I snuck out for the day with my friend, my dad grounded me for the entire summer. This experience led to resentment, but it didn't instill a lesson about seeking permission; it taught me how to avoid getting caught in the future. This highlights an unintended consequence of punishment in parenting teens—it encourages resourcefulness in avoiding consequences without addressing the underlying issues.

Punishment is not an effective method for teaching new behaviors. Instead, it creates discord and long-lasting resentment in relationships. People often remember how others treated them more clearly than the specific behavior that resulted in the punishment. Therefore, if your goal is to strengthen your relationship with your teen and promote corrective learning, punishment is an ill-advised approach.

Sometimes frequent punishment conditions teens to

punish themselves. They think that feeling sad or upset means they deserve punishment. This doesn't mean parents are at fault if a teen self-harms, but a regular pattern of harsh responses can contribute to teens being tough on themselves in unhealthy ways.

Teach Positive Opposites

Encouraging and reinforcing positive behaviors that counter self-destructive behaviors can replace harmful impulses with healthier options. It's essential to teach skills that correspond to both the function and intensity of the problematic behavior. This approach involves understanding the emotional needs driving the behavior and introducing positive behaviors that satisfy these same needs. Positive coping strategies might include mindfulness, physical activity, artistic outlets, or Seeking Support from a friend or therapist. By nurturing these skills and rewarding their application, your teen can learn new, beneficial methods to manage their emotions, reducing the tendency toward self-destructive behaviors.

For example, to counteract your teen's episodes of anger, you might reinforce alternative behaviors. If your teen channels their anger into taking deep breaths, counting to ten, or effectively using "I" statements to convey their emotions, you should positively reinforce these actions.

My teen didn't go to school for a good six months. At first, they'd fight or run or lock themselves in their room. And then with therapy and skills, they learned how to Notice and Name their emotions. They learned how to use Cope & Cool Down skills. Despite not arriving at school on time, they were talking to me more frequently about their challenges. I made it a point to reinforce every instance of communication, practicing the principles of shaping and incremental progress. By reinforcing alternative behaviors, you're helping your teen learn to replace their behavior with more appropriate ways of expressing their emotions.

THE 5-TO-1 RULE

That summer I spent in my room after sneaking out for the day, I listened a lot to The Doors. The lyrics of Jim Morrison's "5 to 1" left a lasting impression on me, and it's how I think about the concept of reinforcement in the parent-teen dynamic too.

With the 5-to-1 Rule, aim to balance every criticism or correction directed at your teen with at least five positive reinforcements. This helps build a positive relationship between parent and teen and creates a supportive environment for your teen to develop new, positive behaviors.

Think of it as a game of "hotter or colder." I'm thinking of an object in the room, and when I say "colder," it means you're moving away from the object. But it doesn't give you any clear direction on how to find it. When I say "warmer" or "hotter," it means you're getting closer. By frequently providing positive feedback, I'm reinforcing your progress toward finding the object.

This feedback loop is important because it helps you stay motivated and on track. When you know you're moving in the right direction, it gives you a sense of accomplishment and a desire to continue. It's the same in many aspects of life, whether it's learning a new skill, working toward a goal, or improving relationships.

The key to understanding why a behavior persists is in looking at the reinforcers that occur during or within seconds of when the behavior occurs. This can help you identify the function of the behavior and how to increase or decrease it. In my own self-harm as a teen, this behavior was reinforced by short-term relief from emotional pain and long-term social and emotional connection. Understanding behaviorism allows you to foster healthy behaviors in your teen and diminish harmful ones over time.

TOP TAKEAWAYS

- **Triggering Transactions:** Remember the Transactional Model where triggers and responses interact. Be aware of how you can influence each other.
- **Behavior's Observable Nature:** Behavior encompasses thoughts, actions, and anything observable. It's not just actions, but also internal processes.
- **Consequences Maintain Behavior:** Behaviors are maintained by consequences. Rewards reinforce behaviors, like the high of a drug or the delight of ice cream. Positive reinforcement and negative reinforcement drive behavior changes.
- **Reinforcement and Punishment:** Positive reinforcement involves gaining something desirable. Negative reinforcement is about escaping or avoiding undesirable situations. Punishment, while ineffective in teaching new behaviors, can create discord and resentment. Focus on reinforcing positive opposites instead.
- **Behavioral Strategies:** Employ the 5-to-1 ratio for healthy behaviors, aiming to reinforce preferred actions more than addressing annoying or unhelpful ones. Shaping small steps, using planned ignoring during extinction, and managing extinction bursts are key strategies. Develop a reinforcement schedule, track progress, and be a scientific observer of your behaviors.

THE GROUNDWORK FOR RECONNECTION

All behavior has a function and makes sense. By regulating your emotions, validating your teen's feelings, and reinforcing progress, you can shape their behavior. Once you've established a foundation of trust and respect, it's time to work on rebuilding the relationship and strengthening the bond between you and your teen.

CHAPTER 8

Restore the Relationship and Rebuild the Rubble

MY SISTER INVITED ME TO ATTEND HER FIRST CHILD'S baby shower, a gathering I knew would be filled with family members I hadn't seen in years. After weighing the pros and cons, and giving myself several pep talks, I went. My biggest fear was rejection for being my true self, but I realized this had already happened long ago.

The wildest thing went down. Select family members came up to me. They talked. We laughed. It was the most normal thing in the world. I had so much fun, and I belonged. Best of all—I belonged as the most authentic version of me.

They said, "We love you. We miss you. We wish you'd come back." I felt it, and I loved them back. Yet I left with an anger so deep in my belly from the grief of knowing that I got a glimpse of the life I didn't get to have with the family I believed didn't want me.

Because the context clearly showed that in their version of the story, I wasn't the one who had been told that I wasn't allowed, the one who had been cast out. It was evident that I had been falsely portrayed as malicious. And the grandmother with the globe of white hair who sat at the corner table averting her eyes...she didn't approach me. She didn't set them right.

I didn't choose this path, but I lived through it and learned to accept it. The grief, though, still burns fiercely within me. I wanted a family that didn't want me. Or maybe they wanted me too. It's just...neither of us knew. I didn't choose this. But I lived it. And in the end, we all lost.

I've accepted that I can't control the judgments and reactions of the people around me. I've learned that some relationships are worth revisiting and rebuilding and some are better left as unruffled feathers from a past flock. I've rekindled some connections. I didn't choose what happened, but I can influence what happens next.

This hope for change extends beyond past family dynamics; it's equally applicable to your current relationship with your teen. If you frequently rely on arguing, punishing, or ignoring, consider more effective approaches. It's much easier to pave the way to a close connection now than to repair a rift years later while also grieving what could have been. Trust me. By adopting practices like "Flipping the Script," you can improve your current relationship with your teen. Using the Hierarchy of Connection as a guide, you can strengthen these bonds incrementally. Let's work together to rebuild and restore your relationships, one step at a time.

FLIP THE SCRIPT

Transforming your relationship with your teen is a gradual process. Think about how long you've been stuck in your current interaction patterns. Picture a boulder repeatedly rolling down the same mountain slope, carving a deep path in the soil. This groove propels the boulder along the familiar route, allowing it to descend rapidly and smoothly. To change its course, you must resist the boulder's tendency to follow the old path and instead continuously roll it along a new one. This involves recognizing the pull toward the familiar (even when it's unproductive) and actively striving to act differently to achieve a new result.

Acting opposite of your urges can lead to surprising results. It opens possibilities and shifts you out of mood-dependent behavior. The Flip the Script skill involves acting opposite to your immediate impulses and starts with Noticing and Naming your emotion. Every emotion has an urge that comes with it. Sadness often leads to withdrawal, anxiety to avoidance, and anger to lashing out. These are the mood-dependent behaviors tied to your feelings.

Each time Sadie entered a room, her father Will's demeanor would shift, turning closed off and irritable. This response, a pattern since Sadie snuck out with Will's car a few months back, sparked anxiety in her, causing her shoulders to tense and her stance to become defensive. Her often curt and irritated replies only heightened the tension, as Will perceived this behavior as disrespectful. This pattern presented a significant barrier to developing a closer relationship, a goal both Sadie and her parents expressed during therapy sessions.

Acting opposite to our impulses is helpful when we seek to change outcomes, regulate our emotions, or transform experiences. Often, our emotions are reasonable—mourning the transition from the child we knew to the teenager we're getting to know is understandable. We wouldn't want to alter this; it's a natural and necessary process. However, snapping at your teen, leading to both of you storming out of the room, isn't constructive. It obstructs the path to a stronger bond with your teen. The goal is to change our reactions when our emotions and impulses are valid but lead to damaging or ineffective behaviors, or when the emotion itself is unfounded and we need to cultivate a healthier response.

When deciding whether to use the Flip the Script skill, envision the outcome of your actions. Play the whole mental movie in your mind. Ask yourself: If you give in to your emotion, will it bring you closer to your goals? Will it be beneficial? If not, then taking the opposite action is your best course.

Instead of nagging your teen to complete homework for hours on end, try a more constructive approach. For instance, ask, "Can I help you create flashcards to study for chemistry?" Then, sit at the table with them. Instead of resorting to criticism or confrontation, consider changing your response to transform the entire interaction, which has the potential to lead to a different, more positive outcome.

RESIST THE URGE TO SNOOP

With sensitive issues, direct questions are preferable to snooping or probing. Respectful and straightforward communication paves the way for stronger connections and avoids unnecessary conflict.

The impulse to seek answers through invasion of privacy stems from a place of desperation—a parent's quest to ease their teen's anguish. But such actions often backfire, highlighting the critical need for open dialogue and mutual respect. This was the case for Lauren and Mike with their sixteen-year-old daughter, Hattie.

Lauren and Mike had been noticing changes in their daughter's behavior—she seemed more secretive and less communicative. Out of concern, they read her diary while she was out with friends. As they turned the pages, they found detailed accounts of Hattie experimenting with alcohol and substances.

Reacting with a mix of fear, anger, and disappointment, Lauren and Mike confronted Hattie that evening. They disregarded her privacy and focused on their shock and disapproval. The conversation erupted with accusations and shouting.

Hattie felt completely betrayed. The diary was her private space, a place for her thoughts and feelings, never meant for her parents' eyes. The breach of trust was profound. Hattie shut down, responding with silence or short retorts. The dynamic in the household dramatically shifted. The parents' intention to protect their daughter had unknowingly damaged their relationship.

Lauren and Mike's discovery and the ensuing confrontation did little to address Hattie's substance use. Their actions eroded the trust that is foundational to open communication and guidance. Hattie no longer felt safe sharing her thoughts or seeking advice from her parents. She relied more on her peers, some of whom were part of the behaviors her parents feared.

I have never understood more than in my experience of parenting a depressed teen why some parents will read texts and diaries and snoop around. You feel lost and left out, and you're looking for *any* answer that will give you the way to fix your teen's suffering.

But the truth remains that this is not your journey, and you cannot live in your teen's body and brain for them. You can only hold, guide, and provide the safety net they need without completely shattering them.

When you notice the urge to snoop, go back to the Feel Your Feelings skill. This is a practice in learning to tolerate your own anxiety and uncertainty. It completely sucks, but you can handle it. Your teen will more likely trust you and want to talk to you when you give them the space to come to you rather than being caught by you.

DITCH THE TRAINING WHEELS

Ollie was a teen who felt extremely anxious about joining our skills group. They were worried that no one would like them and that others might find them weird. After some encouragement, they agreed to give it a shot. Ollie attended the first session, and when they came back the following week, they felt disappointed. "No one liked me," they said. "I knew it wouldn't work."

We took a moment to explore what had happened. They admitted, "I was there, but I played on my phone the whole time, and nobody talked to me. It felt awkward." So I asked if they had really immersed themselves in the experience, allowed themselves to be visible, and actively participated. Truly flipping the script on their anxiety would have meant diving in full force. However, by playing on their phone the whole time, they appeared withdrawn and disengaged to the group, inadvertently validating their own fears: "No one was talking to me; they must have thought I was strange."

For flipping the script in your relationship with your teen, remember that for this approach to work, you must be willing to immerse yourself into new situations and let go of the need to keep your training wheels on just in case things don't go as planned. This can be a vulnerable process, but the potential for increased connection and understanding makes it worth it.

PARENT LIKE A THERAPIST

Practicing mindfulness and acting opposite to your conditioned responses will improve your relationship with your teen and lead to a closer connection with them.

Your thoughts, emotions, and behaviors intertwine in a cyclical manner. After repeated conflicts, you and your teen might avoid one another. If you consistently steer clear of your teen, you miss out on chances for positive interactions that could mend the relationship. Your teen might interpret your avoidance as disinterest and react with their own set of emotions, thoughts, and actions. Relationship patterns are reciprocal. Using the Flip the Script technique can be an impactful step in reenergizing your connection with your teen.

FLIP THE SCRIPT, STEP BY STEP

Start by actively seeking moments to engage with your teen, aiming to establish a healthier dynamic. Note your reactions when your teen enters the room. Do you become tense? Does your heart rate increase? Observe their behavior, reactions, and interactions too. Remember that as a parent, you lead by example. Recognize and assume responsibility for transforming the moment. Stay genuine—don't force it. Acknowledge your instinctive reactions and affirm your dedication to strengthening the relationship. Imagine how you might respond differently. Visualize it until it feels natural, so that when you're in that moment, your response is authentic.

CHOOSE YOUR TARGET

As mentioned before, it's important to focus on just one target at a time. When choosing your focus, ask yourself: what is one behavior you would like to change?

PINPOINT THE EMOTION, IMPULSE, AND ALTERNATIVE ACTION

With your chosen focus in mind, consider the emotions and impulses that surface in that context. What feelings arise that leave you anxious, frustrated, or overwhelmed? How do you usually react to these emotions? Now, what would be a constructive, opposite action you could take?

For instance, if you want to refrain from reacting with visible shock and sadness when you see your teen's self-harm scars, and instead provide support that doesn't cause them feelings of shame, begin by envisioning your usual response. This may include gasping, crying, and focusing intensely on their scars. Notice the familiar tightness in your throat and the fear-induced stiffness in your body. Now reimagine the scene. As you see the scar again, take a deliberate inhale, channeling empathy for your teen's pain. Additionally, envision granting yourself a moment of compassion.

CREATE A MENTAL MOVIE OF THE SITUATION

Holding your chosen focus and action plan in mind, craft a detailed mental movie of the situation you're preparing for. Picture the moment you encounter your target—perhaps it's seeing your teen try on their prom dress, the pale pink and white scars crisscrossing her arm coming into view. Strive to make this mental imagery vivid and lifelike, engaging all your senses to form a distinct visual in your mind.

VISUALIZE YOURSELF RESPONDING DIFFERENTLY

Identify where you can Flip the Script to change the story's outcome. With the mental scene set, envision a new way of responding. Picture yourself employing your new techniques, like slow, deep breaths and gradual muscle relaxation. See your expression as tranquil, your eyes soft, and a gentle smile just beginning to form. As you rehearse, vividly fill in all the details—the people present, the environment, and the potential results of your changed reaction.

REFINE THROUGH REPETITION

Solidify your alternative approach by repeating this visualization regularly. Dedicate a few minutes daily to rehearsing your alternative response to the chosen scenario in your mind. You might also set aside time to write the new version of the scenario on paper. Read it aloud and record yourself. Listen to this recording as you fall asleep at night. With consistent repetition, you'll gain confidence and ease in applying this skill when it matters in real life.

THE HIERARCHY OF CONNECTION

When you're adept at recognizing your emotions, understanding your impulses, and feeling empowered to regulate your response, you're prepared to enhance your relationship using the Hierarchy of Connection. This comprises three mindful methods for spending quality time with your teen, each a stepping stone in increasing the strength of your bond.

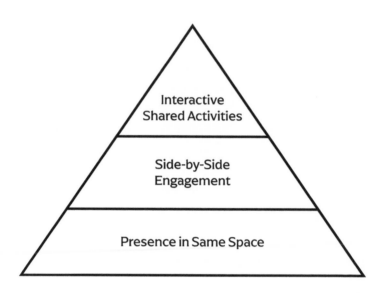

PRESENCE IN THE SAME SPACE

Begin by sharing a room with your teen, each of you involved in separate activities. Perhaps they're engrossed in YouTube while you're putting away groceries. You're sharing the space without conflict or avoidance. This is the initial step, a gentle introduction to the realm of connection. Once you can coexist peacefully, you're ready for the next level.

SIDE-BY-SIDE ENGAGEMENT

The second step involves taking part in a shared, passive activity. It could be something like watching a show on Netflix or sitting together during a car ride. You're both part of the same activity but not interacting with each other. Achieve this step without disputes, and you're set for the last phase.

INTERACTIVE SHARED ACTIVITIES

The ultimate stage of connection is interactive and reciprocal. This is where you and your teen engage in something together, such as having a dinner conversation or playing a board game. It facilitates a meaningful connection, allowing both of you to share an experience. Interaction doesn't always mean conversation; my own teen isn't much for talking and deflects direct questions but will happily join me in playing music. Through this, we find connection rather than frustration. Understand what resonates with your teen and plays to your combined strengths.

Start small, mastering each step before progressing. Start by sending a text. Take your teen for a drive to see friends. Allow them to pick the music in the car. Say yes when you can to requests. The more successes you build at each stage, the more connection and trust you rebuild.

When you've established a reciprocal rapport with your teen, aim to continuously gather positive experiences. Develop a weekly dining ritual or enjoy spontaneous moments of togetherness. Cherish these times, yet stay grounded in your expectations.

Teenagers instinctively shift their focus away from family time toward independence—it's not personal; it's developmental. Embrace this change with Radical Acceptance. As your child matures, they're programmed to distance themselves from you, which is a normal part of their growth. Manage your emotions around this phase with your own coping skills.

Reflect on your fondest family memories. Often, they're small moments: shared jokes, mishaps that turned into stories. These are the golden opportunities to connect with your teen. It's the significance, not the size, that leaves an imprint. Simple activities, like walking the dog or watching a favorite show together, lay the bricks for a rebuilt relationship. The effort you put in now is an investment in a trusting, enduring bond that extends beyond their teenage years.

Understanding relationship limitations is also crucial. Not everyone will connect on a deep level, and that's okay. It took me until my thirties to realize my father's interactions with me had their limits. We found common ground working on renovations for teen support centers. While our relationship may not be based on reciprocity—his capacity doesn't allow for it—I've learned to accept and enjoy our side-by-side connection. This acceptance has paved the way for the strongest connection possible between us.

TOP TAKEAWAYS

- **Acting Opposite to Urges:** Acting against your natural urges can lead to unexpected positive outcomes. This approach breaks mood-dependent behavior patterns and opens up new possibilities.
- **Mindful Response Transformation:** Shift away from conditioned reactions like arguing or punishing. Practicing mindfulness and choosing intentional responses can significantly improve your relationship with your teen.
- **Changing Patterns Takes Time:** Just like a boulder creates a groove over time, changing relationship dynamics requires consistent effort and intentional choices. Patience is key in creating new, positive patterns.
- **Flip the Script Skill:** Start by recognizing and naming your emotions. Challenge mood-dependent behaviors to make positive choices. Visualization and repetition are effective tools for implementing change.
- **Mindful Connection:** Reconnect with your teen, progressing from sharing the same space to engaging in interactive activities. Build small successes over time to rebuild trust and connection.

REBUILDING STEP BY STEP

Rebuilding a relationship requires patience. Begin with manageable steps, concentrating on behaviors and interactions that pave the way to your larger aspiration—one brick at a time. Choosing to rebuild is deliberate, demanding effort and enduring pain, thus calling upon your deepest mindfulness and regulation abilities. In my experience, it was only through mourning the absence of twelve years that I could forge a genuine reconnection. You possess the skills. Now, let's activate the plan to maintain progress.

Conclusion

Check the Burners before
Bed for Best Results

WHEN YOU SURROUND YOURSELF WITH AN ENVIRON-
ment that affirms and validates, you become your best self.
The opposite holds true as well. Parenting a Fire Feeler is an
ongoing process that requires intentional effort, awareness,
and consistent action. It's a journey, not a destination. When
you understand the interplay of biology and the environment,
when you learn to regulate, validate, reinforce, and rebuild,
you will set yourself up for success in a healthy relationship
with your teen.

Your teen's behaviors often serve as coping mechanisms
for emotional distress. To address them effectively, it's crucial
to understand the underlying reasons behind these behaviors.
By identifying the root causes, you can gain insight into how
to approach and work toward finding solutions.

One valuable way to support your teen throughout this
process is by practicing mindfulness. This can involve daily

activities like finding moments of stillness, focusing on your breath, or observing your thoughts and emotions without passing judgment. Self-judgment and judgments about your teen can intensify emotions and create obstacles to effective communication. By cultivating a nonjudgmental mindset daily, you can better regulate your emotional responses and remain a consistent, supportive presence for your teen.

It's important to acknowledge that grieving is ongoing and lifelong. Just when you believe you've moved past a challenging experience, new events, phrases, or situations can reopen old wounds. Be prepared for such moments and have strategies in place for navigating them.

Above all, validation serves as the initial step toward change. To address a problem, you must first acknowledge its existence. By validating your teen's experiences and emotions, you create a secure and supportive environment for them to explore and address their behaviors.

Another critical step is reinforcing what's effective. Just as you need to Feed the Meter to keep a parking spot, it's vital to regularly acknowledge and reinforce positive behaviors in your Fire Feeler. By continually validating and reinforcing what works, you can help boost their confidence and encourage them to continue on a positive path.

Last, it's essential to prioritize repairing relationships when conflicts arise. This entails being willing to put in the effort to resolve issues and rebuild trust. By approaching conflicts with openness and a willingness to work through them, you can establish a stronger and more resilient relationship with your teen.

Effective parenting is no different than mastering a musical instrument. It's not a one-and-done process and requires a continuous commitment to deliberate practice. This means being intentional about practicing the skills outlined in this book and observing where and when they are most needed. As you apply these skills in your daily life, take time to notice their impact. Reflect on what worked and what didn't, and why.

DELIBERATE PRACTICE DAILY LOG

Supporting Karen in our parent group, I helped her implement an assertiveness script with her teen. Initially, Karen reported the script wasn't effective and led to frustration. Upon further examination, the failure wasn't in the skill itself, but in its application.

Her teen was fully immersed in another task, their focus diverted, which made them less receptive to Karen's approach. Karen's tone carried a sense of anxiety and urgency, which interfered with the effectiveness of her message.

Karen's experience is a valuable lesson: successful interactions with teenagers require the right blend of skill, context, and emotional awareness. Regularly practicing the techniques in this book is essential for success. Consider seeking feedback from therapy or a parent group to help you stay on track.

To support the continuous process of deliberate practice, I have developed a tracking form. This form serves as a daily practice log, and it includes every skill discussed in this book. It provides space for you to note when and how you applied each skill, your observations regarding its effectiveness, and your thoughts on potential improvements.

Place a checkmark in the corresponding space for the day you practiced a particular skill. Take a moment to reflect on what worked well and what didn't and consider how you can improve your approach in the future. To download a printable version of this form, please visit www.creativehealingphilly.com/book.

SKILL	SUN	MON	TUES	WED	THURS	FRI	SAT
Notice & Name w/o Judgment							
Cope & Cool Down							
Feel Your Feelings							
Proactive Self-Care Skills							
Radical Acceptance							
Seeking Support							
Validation							
DIFFERENT							
Flip the Script							
Hierarchy of Connection							
Notes							

Change doesn't happen overnight. It requires patience, persistence, and, most importantly, consistent practice. By using the tracking form daily, you can monitor your progress, and see the tangible results of your efforts.

Through this systematic approach, you'll find that the skills become more natural and intuitive, weaving them gradually into the fabric of your everyday life. The transformation might be gradual, but the results—a harmonious home and a healthy, thriving teen—will be profound and lasting.

You've got this. I believe in you. I'm rooting for you.

Glossary of Terms

5-to-1 Rule: This rule suggests for every one criticism or correction offered, five reinforcing statements should be provided. This approach aims to build positive relationships and self-esteem by ensuring that positive interactions substantially outnumber negative ones.

Biosocial Theory: In Dialectical Behavior Therapy (DBT), this refers to the theory that emotional vulnerability results from both biological factors (such as brain chemistry) and social experiences (such as upbringing and environment).

Blame & Shame Continuum: The tendency to either blame oneself or shift blame to others when avoiding an emotional experience, often as a way of deflecting from the emotions.

Cope & Cool Down: Immediate coping skills used to regulate emotions and bring them back to a manageable level during moments of heightened emotional intensity.

DIFFERENT: A behavior management system broken down as follows:

- **Duration:** How long the behavior lasts.
- **Intensity:** How strong the behavior is.
- **Frequency:** How often the behavior occurs.
- **Feed the Meter:** Identifying what reinforces or fuels the behavior.
- **Escape the Pain:** How the behavior helps avoid emotional discomfort.
- **Remove Reinforcers:** Identifying and eliminating factors that encourage the behavior.
- **Extinction Planning:** Strategies for reducing or eliminating the behavior.
- **Natural Consequences:** The outcomes that naturally follow a behavior, used to understand and modify future behavior.
- **Teach Positive Opposites:** Providing alternative behaviors.

Dialectical Behavior Therapy (DBT): A therapeutic model designed by Marsha Linehan, focused on helping individuals manage and regulate emotions, cope with stress, improve relationships, and live mindfully.

Emotion Dysregulation: Difficulty in managing and responding to emotional experiences, often resulting in emotional reactions that are challenging to control.

Extinction Cope Ahead Plan: A structured strategy to prepare for behavior change by anticipating challenges, reactions, and coping strategies in advance during the process of behavior extinction.

Feel Your Feelings: The practice of mindfully experiencing emotions without judgment, allowing yourself to fully feel and acknowledge your emotions.

Fire Feeler: A sensitive individual who experiences emotions quickly, is prone to impulsive behaviors, and has emotions that are long-lasting and take a long time to return to emotional balance.

Flip the Script: The practice of intentionally engaging in actions that are contrary to one's emotional impulses in a situation, with the purpose of achieving a different and more desirable outcome.

Hierarchy of Connection: A three-step process for increasing the level of connection and interaction with loved ones. It starts with being able to share space, progresses to passive shared activities, and culminates in interactive activities.

Judgments: Labeling experiences, people, or oneself in a rigid and often negative manner, forming fixed opinions or assessments that can be harsh.

Name Skill: The ability to articulate or label one's experiences or emotions with words, putting emotions and experiences into verbal expression.

Notice Skill: The skill of observing an experience or emotion without verbalizing or attaching judgments to it, just being aware of the emotion or experience without adding commentary.

Primary Emotions: Basic emotions experienced in response to an event, such as fear, anger, sadness, or joy. These are the initial emotional reactions to a situation.

Radical Acceptance: This term, originating from the Dialectical Behavior Therapy (DBT) model, refers to the act of completely and totally accepting an experience, often accompanied by a process of grieving, and allowing yourself to fully acknowledge and come to terms with the reality of a situation.

Reinforcement: A technique used to encourage a behavior by offering a positive reward (positive reinforcement) or removing an unpleasant experience (negative reinforcement). This method helps increase the likelihood that the desired behavior will occur again.

Scented Candle Skills/Self-Care: Proactive Self-Care skills used to reduce the likelihood of powerful reactions and emotion-driven behaviors.

Secondary Emotions: Emotions that come from thoughts and judgments, making emotions more complicated than just a natural response, often stemming from how one interprets and evaluates Primary Emotions.

Seeking Support: The process of creating a support system, including friends, family, and professionals, reaching out to others for emotional help.

Shaping Plan: A behavioral term referring to molding or guiding an individual's behavior toward a desired outcome through reinforcement for each small step.

Transactional Model: A term coined by Dr. Alan Fruzetti to describe relationships and how each person both triggers and reinforces the other, showing that all individuals exist within a system of others that influence their actions.

Validation: The acknowledgment and acceptance of another person's feelings, thoughts, behaviors, and experiences as understandable, offering validation to others as a way of acknowledging their emotions and experiences.

Acknowledgments

IN CREATING THIS BOOK, I'VE DRAWN STRENGTH AND inspiration from the following individuals, each profoundly influencing my life and contributing significantly to the pages of this work.

K, you transformed my world the moment you were on your way. You became my beacon, guiding me toward regulation, health, and the true embodiment of the skills I advocate. You are the heart of my why.

Adam, you were the mirror reflecting a version of myself I dared to believe in. Your partnership and support have been my constant in a sea of change. I am immensely grateful for you.

Maureen, in creating your family, you rekindled my connection to what having one means.

Your family means the world to me, and I'm filled with hope for the generational healing that offers a brighter future for our children.

Lauren, through our journey from the "wrong side of the tracks" and back, we've remained thick as thieves. Thank you for always being there.

To my parents, there are no villains in our story, only individuals doing their best with the skills they had. You taught me resilience, albeit in ways you never intended, and through this, I learned to be skillful and to thrive.

To my father, I once believed my success was fueled by a desire to make you proud. Along the way, I discovered the power in standing strong for myself, not just in response to you. This book, the one that might have helped guide us years ago, is now a reality. Challenge met.

To my incredible Creative Healing team, your dedication and passion have been pivotal. Together, we've implemented these strategies, understanding their impact firsthand. I am proud to work alongside you each day, making a difference in the lives of teens and parents.

And finally, to my DBT community, your principles have been the compass for this book. Special thanks to Shaelene Kite and Kathryn Butts for training my team and being pillars of support in fortifying these strategies.

About the Author

KATIE K. MAY, LPC, owner and executive director of Creative Healing, is a national speaker and trainer specializing in therapy for teens with depression, self-harm, and suicidal thoughts. As one of only eleven Linehan board-certified Dialectical Behavior Therapy (DBT) clinicians in Pennsylvania, she's an expert in this gold-standard treatment for life-threatening behaviors. Katie is committed to helping teens feel accepted for who they are while teaching them skills to build a life they love. She graduated from Villanova University and West Chester University of Pennsylvania and resides in the Philadelphia area with her family and Boston Terrier, Penny. To learn more about Katie and her work, visit www.creativehealingphilly.com.

9 781544 545592